10)22

HarperCollins Publishers
77-85 Fulham Palace Road
London
W6 8JB

www.collins.co.uk

Collins is a registered trademark of
HarperCollins Publishers Ltd.

A catalogue record for this book is
available from the British Library.

10 9 8 7 6 5 4 3 2 1

ISBN 978-0-00-729799-3

Printed and bound in Italy by Rotolito

Collins uses papers that are natural,
renewable and recyclable products
made from wood grown in sustainable
forests. The manufacturing processes
conform to the environmental
regulations of the country of origin.

THiS BOOK
BELONGS to

....

....

Kate
AND
GiN

Kate AND GIN

Collins

Learn to Dance and
Do Tricks with
Kate and Gin
Stars of
Britain's Got Talent

CONTENTS

MEETING GIN

I was born in August 1991 into a home filled with animals. I suppose because I grew up with a lot of pets I developed a sort of natural relationship with them, but I especially loved our dogs – Mum even thinks I am part dog! And of course, it wasn't long before I was desperate to have a puppy of my own.

We used to have a naughty little Welsh Terrier called Merlin. All Welsh Terriers are pretty naughty actually, but he was a lot of fun, always biting at trouser legs and causing a commotion of some sort. Along with Merlin we had half a zoo of creatures roaming around: a little gosling that used to follow me everywhere like a dog, a Shetland pony, chickens, a horse, sheep and I even had a hamster of my own. Looking back, it was a kind of training for me to look after my hamster, after all, if I couldn't care for a hamster, then what chance did I have with a dog? Yet I never saw cleaning his cage or feeding him as a chore – I loved looking after him as I did with all our animals.

I enjoyed going to dog shows with Mum and my sister, but while they preferred show breeding and grooming, I found myself fascinated by the agility shows. The more I watched them, the more I began to wish that I could train a dog of my own to do those impressive obstacle courses. Our family mainly kept Welsh Terriers, so I think I surprised Mum when I pleaded for a Border Collie. Quite simply, I had noticed that Border Collies were generally the best dogs for agility training, and I wanted one!

Our first idea was to visit the Dogs Trust at Roden in Shropshire where we found a beautiful Springer Spaniel

IT WAS A WONDERFUL MOMENT, MEETING MY OWN DOG

called Logan, who I adored. He was so lively and he kept bringing toys to the door for us; such a friendly dog. Unfortunately, our enquiries revealed that the police wanted to adopt him as a sniffer dog, and we regretfully decided that he'd probably prefer to be a proper working dog rather than a pet.

I was still desperate for my own dog, but for a while we didn't seem to make any progress. However, Mum and Dad were still secretly discussing the issue and one day close to my 10th birthday, they sneaked away to a farm that had some Border Collie pups for sale while I was at school. And that's where they found Gin. She was so excitable and friendly, as if she was demanding to go home with them. I think Mum and Dad were left with no choice!

When I came home that day I remember saying to Mum that I could hear Merlin making some strange noises. Mum smiled and led me into the kitchen, and there was Gin, only a tiny puppy, just a few weeks old. I fell in love with her straight away. It was a wonderful moment, meeting my own dog, and it was such a surprise too. Gin, of course, has been absolutely everything I could have wished for. She's naughty, she's always on the go and always wants to play, but I always feel so lucky to have this amazing dog as my best friend.

They say that I'm not the prettiest Border
Collie on the block. Well, I say, looks don't
matter when you can dance. And so here I
am, a canine celebrity, queen of the kennel.
But don't get me wrong. I'm not conceited
or a dancing diva like Ant and Dec said I was. I know that
you cannot reach the A-list without lots of hard work
and that's exactly what we do – work. We train harder
than all the other *Britain's Got Talent* winners combined.
While George Sampson and Signature were strutting
their stuff, Kate and I were training in the garden in
Nantwich. For hours and hours every single day. I don't
know what I would do without the training. I've been
told I put the H in hyper and have more energy than a
thousand dogs. But you need it to reach the standards
that we have reached.

When I think of who else has performed in front
of Simon Cowell all over the world, from Bon Jovi to
Barry Manilow, it's just mind boggling. But I tried not to

think about it on that amazing night before the panel of judges and that wonderful audience. I had a job to do and I wanted to do it to the best of my ability. To please Kate if nothing else. I have to say that I will never forget the moment when Simon Cowell said: 'I've been looking for Lassie all my life and I've found him!' It was overwhelming. But then something started to niggle. While it was a very nice thing to say Simon, and I don't want to sound churlish here, all Lassie had to do was run in and out of rooms and bark a bit. Lassie couldn't dance. And there were lots of Lassies in the end. But there's only one Kate.

Kate is the reason why I'm here now. Kate is my life and without her I would be nothing. Behind every canine celebrity there is a great trainer and Kate is it. She was the one who told me not to shred slippers when I was a puppy. She was the one who tempered my instincts when I had the urge to run out of puppy training classes. If it hadn't been for Kate I might have been cautioned by the local Bobby for jumping over the fence and stealing the bread left by the neighbours for the birds. There's no end of trouble that I might have gotten into. I know I was described as a difficult dog by Kate's mother. So who knows how it could have ended up. But she channelled all this energy into the star I am now. I know I wasn't easy.

But I want to reassure my growing number of fans that I won't let all this go to my head or end up in kennel rehab for a refresher course on basic discipline.

I know I have love to keep me going and that is in the form of my beloved Kate.

Chapter One
OWNiNG a DOG

Choosing the Right Dog for You

My relationship with Gin over the last few years has been extremely rewarding and I think it's obvious to any observer how much we adore each other's company. The idea of owning a dog can be very attractive, especially for children, and having a loyal companion, a friend and a confidante is a wonderful thing. Owning a dog carries huge responsibilities, but if you are willing to put in that time and effort, as I have with Gin, the results can be enriching.

Gin – My Perfect Match

Unlike some pets, the breed you choose is absolutely vital. Gin came from a family that were experienced in breeding Border Collies. She was young when I first met her, but she had been treated well and had been given a pleasant start to life. Collies have been bred to round up sheep, so not only are they animals that love almost endless exercise and relish plenty of play, they actually need a high level of physical activity in order to be happy. Gin has always been remarkably energetic and while part of that is related to her personality, a lot is simply due to her breed.

Gin was a perfect match for me because I love to be active, especially outside, and fortunately I have the energy to keep up with Gin's demands! During *Britain's Got Talent* one or two newspaper columnists wondered whether it was cruel for Gin to have been taught so many tricks. Such comments only highlight the ignorance of the writers. Collies, like all working dogs such as gun dogs (Golden Retrievers or Labrador Retrievers, for example), or herding dogs (Collies or Sheepdogs), need a lot of exercise. They thrive on it. Although they make fantastic pets, they love to work, to be occupied and to have a purpose.

We have another beautiful Collie that we adopted from a rescue home. Originally, she lived in a flat in London, but was given up by owners who said they couldn't cope. Collies are bred to run for miles every day, so it makes sense that she would not have been happy cooped up in a flat with no room to stretch and burn off energy. It's simply not fair on a Collie to expect it to be happy in that sort of environment, which is a great example of why you should take great care when selecting a breed.

WHICH BREED SUITS YOU?

A careful examination of your lifestyle will help lead you towards the perfect breed for you. Ask yourself a few straightforward questions:

- Do you have a lot of space in the house?
- Do you have a garden and if so, what size?
- What are you looking for from your dog?
- Will you enjoy a lot of exercise and play with the dog?
- Or are you looking for a more docile companion?

You can disregard many breeds by using some common sense. If you live in a small house or flat, it wouldn't be fair on the dog to choose a large breed such as a Doberman or a Dalmatian. If you are after a dog that doesn't require too much exercise, start by investigating smaller breeds such as Chihuahuas or Pekingese.

If there are young children in the home, then it's advisable to think about how your new dog will integrate into the family. All dogs can be trained and plenty of breeds enjoy the company of children, but very young children should always be supervised around their pet and educated to respect him.

Here are a few examples of breeds that love to play and bond with kids, although this list is by no means exhaustive:

Spaniel	There are many types of Spaniel, including Cocker, Cavalier King Charles and Springer. All are gentle and good with children.
Golden Retriever	A great dog that is always a good choice for families. Blue Peter dogs are often Retrievers (Lucy is the current one), because they are clever and very friendly.
Boxer	Boxers are a lot of fun and full of energy. They love to play with children but they can be a little too exuberant for toddlers.
Border Collie	Obviously I am in a position to heartily recommend these wonderfully intelligent dogs, but with the warning that they do need a great deal of exercise and play.
Dalmatian	All kids love Dalmatians thanks to the films, and these are affectionate family dogs. They can grow quite large and need plenty of exercise, so make sure you have space.
Labrador Retriever	Like the Golden Retriever, the Lab is a reliable choice for a family and loves to play with kids.
Welsh Terrier	My family has bred these lovely dogs for years. They are loving pets, but, again, need serious amounts of exercise and mental stimulation.
Poodle	Poodles come in three sizes – toy, miniature and standard. They train easily and are loyal, beautiful and friendly dogs.

BE HONEST

When you begin your research it's easy to start feeling a little selfish. For example, you might prefer a dog with a shorter coat that doesn't need too much grooming. This is not selfishness, it's being practical. It will do no good for you or a dog if you fall in love with its personality but find you don't have sufficient time to look after its needs.

Exercise, grooming and feeding are all fundamental to the wellbeing of a dog, but don't forget about love! Before Mum and Dad gave me Gin, we came close to taking a Springer Spaniel from a rescue home. They are playful and affectionate but thrive on attention and constant, tender, loving care. If you live a busy life be honest with yourself and don't choose a breed such as the Springer Spaniel – leave him or her to another family who can lavish it with the love it needs.

CROSSBREEDS AND MONGRELS

We shouldn't forget about crossbreeds (where parentage is known) and mongrels (where it is not). A pedigree can be expensive and if you are simply looking for a loving dog for the family, then there's absolutely no reason why you shouldn't decide on a crossbreed.

There are practical advantages. A crossbreed is the product of a larger gene pool and therefore may well be immune to more diseases than pedigree dogs. However, it is worth finding out as much as you can about the dog's ancestry so that you can make the best possible judgement about the temperament of the dog, which can change with age. And if you decide your mongrel deserves to be rewarded for its behaviour and beauty, there's even a national dog show for crossbreeds these days: Scruffts!

INDIVIDUAL PERSONALITIES

Once you've made the decision on the breed, you are left with the even more difficult problem of finding and then choosing your dog. At least in the early stages of choosing you can reason dispassionately about the breed. But once you're into the business of picking your pet, the prospect of dozens of pairs of appealing eyes looking up at you can be a little daunting!

Here are a few tips of what to look out for:

- When Mum and Dad picked out Gin there were three puppies to choose from. However, Gin was the liveliest and the most outgoing, so it was an easy decision to make. This is fairly standard procedure – the most outgoing dog tends to be happiest and the most comfortable with new faces.
- If you come across a nervous dog, it may turn out to be aggressive. He is protective of himself and therefore unpredictable. To put it simply, if the dog is wagging its tail happily it is probably a good choice – if it is cowering in the corner it is best to look elsewhere.
- Make sure you find out as much as possible about the dog or puppy. Ask questions about the dog's temperament and nature and spend some time with the dog and see how he or she reacts to you. Try and watch the dog interact with other dogs, as this will give a good indication of character.
- Always try and see any puppy with its mother to observe how both of them behave. The best and most professional breeders will always make sure their

puppies are well socialised with people and other dogs, they will have been played with and will have received some early instruction in toilet training.

WHERE TO BUY

There's no need at all to take risks in this area, as there are plenty of safe, reliable and reputable places where you can buy a dog and be sure that it has been well cared for. Sadly, pet shops are not always reliable and neither are adverts you might see in your local newspaper.

- If you know an expert breeder personally that is always handy – they might have some suitable pups or at least will be able to offer some good advice.
- The Kennel Club (see p 154) is a wise first port of call. There is plenty of advice on their website, which also offers a Puppy Sales Register that allows you to search for an accredited breeder for your favoured breed.
- A rewarding option is to share your home with a rescue dog. Puppies are great fun, but they are incredibly mischievous and perhaps you may decide that you would prefer an adult dog. Don't think that all rescue dogs have been mistreated; there are often genuine reasons why dogs have been given to charities such as the Dogs Trust or Battersea Dogs Home.

GINFORMATION!

- *The Kennel Club is an excellent source of information.* *www.thekennelclub.org.uk*
- *Kate is a member of the Young Kennel Club, which is great fun! It offers loads of help and advice and you can join even if you don't have a dog! www.youngkennelclub.co.uk*
- *If you want to adopt a dog from a charity here are some very useful sites.* *Battersea Dogs Home: www.dogshome.org.uk* *Dogs Trust: www.dogstrust.org.uk* *RSPCA: www.rspca.org.uk* *National Animal Welfare Trust: www.nawt.org.uk*

Grooming and Feeding

FEEDING YOUR DOG

It is important for your dog to have both the right amount and the right kind of food. If you are unsure, you can always ask your vet, but the branded foods generally supply plenty of information on the packaging about ingredients and the correct quantities for the breed. Some people prefer to make their own food, but it is very difficult to give your dog everything she needs unless you really know what you're doing! Whatever you decide, always make sure your dog has plenty of fresh water available.

Puppies will need to be fed small quantities of food a few times each day to help them grow and sometimes older dogs need to be fed a couple of times per day as well. A dog should always, wherever possible, be fed by the owner as that is an important part of building a close relationship.

Grooming Your Dog

Grooming should be started at an early age and it will become an enjoyable part of the bonding process between you.

Dogs with longer hair often need to be groomed every day to remove tangles and get rid of dead hairs, while short-haired breeds like Gin will enjoy a good session two or three times per week. I've even heard that stroking and grooming your dog actually helps to de-stress humans as well! There are a variety of brushes available, including combs and different bristle strengths, but suitability depends on the breed.

I find it easiest to use a gentle comb through the hair first, followed by a stronger brushing. You should encourage your dog to sit or stand still if possible so that it is easier to do a nice, thorough job.

CARING FOR GIN

Gin was naughty as a puppy! I don't think I have ever seen a dog with so much boundless energy. If you saw her on *Britain's Got Talent* I think you'll agree that she was wonderfully well behaved, but what you didn't see were the years of training and practice that we have put in together to reach that stage.

It didn't take long to discover that Gin was difficult to contain. She'd always be running around outside when I wanted to bring her inside and she had a habit of chewing things up - anything she could get her teeth into. Clearly, before we could start working on my dream to teach her tricks, we had to work very hard on her basic obedience.

Although I was only ten, I had been around dogs all my life so I was able to use my own experience as well as rely on the advice of my parents, who have owned dogs for many years. But even they were surprised by Gin's hyperactivity! Basic training started quickly. For example, I began teaching her to sit and we made sure that she socialised with our other dogs. Then, once she had ben given all her vaccinations, I began taking her to obedience classes.

The classes were held in a large marquee and Gin would go mad with excitement at seeing all the people and other dogs. Quite often she would behave very well and do a 'stay' or a 'recall' perfectly, but then it would be as if something switched in her head and she'd suddenly think 'Oh, bored now, let's go and find something else to do,' and she would shoot off, out into the field and run around and around.

I think I related well to Gin because as a child I was always on the go too, so I could never be angry with her.

HER PUPPYISH PLAYFULNESS OFTEN LANDED HER IN TROUBLE

She was just mischievous rather than disobedient. Let's put it this way, she wasn't the best-behaved dog in the class! The class took place once a week, but keeping my goal of training Gin in the future in mind, I made sure that we kept working and improving on everything that we had been learning in-between lessons. Her enthusiasm was enormously encouraging and I knew that would stand us in good stead for the journey ahead.

All puppies are curious, but Gin would occasionally frighten me with her adventurous nature. She found a way of jumping up onto our big shed and I'd be terrified that she would fall and break a leg, but she never did. In retrospect it really showed what a natural athlete she was. On other occasions she would jump over our gate and help herself to the bread that the neighbours put out for the birds.

Her energetic puppyish playfulness often landed her in trouble, which just made the basic obedience training all the more important. Until I could control and channel her dazzling energy we could not start to take the next steps that I had been dreaming about.

Let me tell you about my energy. I saw this scary film called *Alien* once and in the film this thing, this alien being, bursts out of the chest of an astronaut. Well, my energy sometimes feels like that – a mass – a bundle of something hot and irrepressible inside of me and I just have to run and run and run until I've run it out of my system. Am I making any sense? Or is it only those who are hyper who truly understand? Don't get me wrong, I don't have ADD (Attention Deficit Disorder) or anything like that. I can concentrate for hours. Now. But in the beginning, I was just this crazed little dervish who couldn't sit still.

We're all a bit like that, us Border Collies. It's why we love to work. We should be at work really. Otherwise we might get depressed or go mad for slippers or cushions or leads. But I do remember those early days of training and it was terrible for me as well as for Kate. Keeping still was my main problem and staying 'on command'. Stay, stay, stay, stay, stay. If I heard it once I heard it a thousand times. But I just couldn't. The hot bundle would burn in my chest and I would just HAVE to go and say hello to the other dogs or run as far away from that marquee as I possibly could. Concrete can be hard for dogs. It hurts our paws and scratches our nails. We

would much rather be on the grass. So any chance I could find, I scampered to the grass. Eventually I would come back to Kate, but sometimes I pretended not to hear her calling me. I just wanted to see what was out there beyond the marquee and the cars and the houses. I yearned for the fields and the animals that I could round up and herd into a corner.

When I was a puppy I loved to get up high so I could see the world beyond the back garden at home. And I had this special talent for scrambling up to the top of the shed. And oh, what a view! All those wonderful green fields with fluffy white sheep gambolling in the long, lush grass. And the smells! The cow parsley, the wild roses and the sharp musky smells of the little animals that I longed to ferret out of their lairs. You have no idea what it's like to have a great sense of smell. And we are talking six times better than any human being. Can you imagine? The most you can get excited about is the vinegar on chips. But for me, every smell is like a separate adventure, a call, a lure to something new and mysterious. And when i was young it was irresistible.

Now, with Kate's help, I have learned to control my basic urges. I can still smell those adventures, and they call out to me, begging me to come and find them, but now I have the discipline to resist the temptation.

Where to House Your Pet

HOUSING YOUR DOG

All our dogs, including Gin, live and sleep in kennels outside the house, but as a family we spend a lot of time with them and they are naturally welcome in the home at all times. Because Gin recognises a difference between the house and her kennel, she is very well behaved when she's inside.

For most people, it is probably best for the dog to live in the house where she can become effectively socialised and fully interact with and become part of the family.

There are a number of different kinds of bed you can buy for your dog, but the key is to offer a warm, cosy area – a basket lined with blankets or a comfy dog bed – that your dog sees as home. A fairly popular choice is to use a covered dog crate. These act as a kind of den and can help make your dog feel warm and secure, but just make sure that you buy a crate big enough to suit your dog!

Kate and Gin's Special Bond

I could not agree more with that famous statement about the dog being man's best friend – as long as the quotation refers to mankind as a whole of course! Gin is my best friend and I'm sure that, in turn, I'm Gin's best friend too. For over seven years we have been together, playing, training, going for walks, practising tricks and honing our routines, all of which has helped us to form a tremendous bond that can never be broken.

Our bond was really forged in those first few months, when we spent hours playing together and getting to know each other. That's not to say that you can't have a lasting bond with an older dog that perhaps you adopted from a rescue home, but in our case I really believe that those early times helped to cement the friendship that we have now.

My mum often says that dogs are totally trustworthy and that, although it sounds odd, it can be a real comfort to tell them your secrets or private feelings. It's not as if they can go and tell anyone, after all! My relationship with Gin has been particularly special as it has been a constant during some difficult times that I have experienced.

Once I had acknowledged my ambitions to train Gin to be good enough to perform at the best agility competitions, I knew I would need total dedication. But the by-product of this single-mindedness was that my friends could not really understand why I was investing so much time in my dog. Eventually they gave up on me because every time they asked if I was coming out I would be busy training Gin or going to a competition. Because a lot of them didn't have pets, I think it was difficult for them to comprehend why Gin was so important to me.

MY FRIENDS COULD NOT REALLY UNDERSTAND WHY I WAS INVESTING SO MUCH TIME IN MY DOG

Sometimes I would get called 'Pedigree' at school, which was hurtful. But I do think that people are now beginning to understand my actions, in part thanks to *Britain's Got Talent*. I think all the finalists in the competition said that they admired my act because I had a dog to worry about as well as myself and I really appreciated that recognition.

I believe if you are going to really excel at something you have to put absolutely everything into it. You have to be willing to sacrifice all kinds of things to achieve your goals. Sometimes the situation at school was hard to deal with, but that is why Gin and I have so much love between us. We have spent so much time together, having fun and building trust, and when I had those problems I could always rely on Gin.

You could see the trust we have developed very clearly on *Britain's Got Talent*. Gin didn't really enjoy sitting on stage with the large audience clapping and cheering, but she did it for me. Ant and Dec made a joke about Gin acting like a diva and making demands backstage about a red carpet for the performance, but the memories of Gin's courage, loyalty and perfect displays on that show will stay with me forever as a demonstration of our friendship.

An academic from Cambridge once wrote a book about dogs who seem to know in advance when their owners are coming home. A lot of sceptics poo-pooed his experiments at the time. Well, let me tell you right now, we know. I have waited for Kate when she was coming home from school so many times and I'm always right on the button with the timing. And it is not just about remembering her daily routine, it is about sensing when she's due. I cannot explain it any other way in human terms, except to say that my sense of smell and hearing are so much more acute than any of you can ever hope to understand that I can just pick up signals from Kate from miles away. And all I do is combine those talents with my intelligence and I can anticipate what she's about to do next.

I also know how upset she gets when she is teased sometimes. And now I am being given this chance to tell my story, I would like to state right here and now that all Kate ever wanted to do was to have fun training me, but it turned into so much more than that. She loved me so much that she could see that if I wasn't going to be worked full time, I was going to be a big bundle of trouble with all my excess energy. And so we worked and worked and worked and I suppose that she wasn't doing the things that normal kids do and I think some of her friends resented her never being around. And they used to call her names like Pedigree. But not every kid grows up with the exact same interests. Kate is different, dedicated and remarkable. Simon Cowell said so.

I do have my circle of competitors, but their owners are usually much older and have been dog trainers for years before finding the right dog for competition freestyle. There aren't too many of us at this standard though. It is just too hard!

One of the most difficult things about performing for TV shows like *Britain's Got Talent* was learning to

cope with the audience. It is nothing like Crufts or any of those other dog shows. There, the audience is so much smaller and so much quieter! In the TV show, they were jumping up and down and screaming and cheering. It was hard to hear what Kate was saying and if we hadn't been over our routine again and again, I don't think I could have done it. I mean, I went into a trance, trying to remember everything she told me and to follow her hand and the tip of the pole in the other. The lights were so hot and the atmosphere so frenzied that I almost lost it a number of times. When we finished there was a huge roar that almost deafened my ears.

Control

I have been fortunate with Gin in that she is a well-behaved dog. As a young puppy she may have been exuberant – come to think of it, she still is! – but she has never been a bad dog, only mischievous. It is important to remember that your dog is your responsibility. Poorly trained dogs can be dangerous, so make sure that your dog is trained to be under your control at all times, particularly when out in public.

LEADER OF THE PACK

Dogs are pack animals, which means it is natural for them to make an assessment of their position within your family group. As the owner of your dog you must make it clear that you are in charge. This can be achieved through a combination of methods, as we shall see, but it is most certainly not achieved through the use of fear and intimidation or by shouting at your dog.

Obedience in dogs comes from respect for their owners. Gin sees me as the leader of our little pack, and because of our friendship and trust in each other I am able to rely on her to behave well at all times - even on stressful occasions, such as dogs shows or in front of television cameras.

Dogs will often not understand why they are being shouted at and this breeds fear and confusion – two emotions that can lead to aggression. Dogs respond to being treated fairly, firmly and with rewards when they act correctly. I never have to shout at Gin - of course, I need to rein her in sometimes, but because of the affection and trust we share, she understands when she has misbehaved without the need for me to raise my voice.

STIMULATION

Quite often, a dog behaves badly due to boredom or lack of exercise. Especially with working breeds, a lack of mental or physical stimulation leads to frustration and ultimately poor behaviour as the dog looks for ways to use up energy.

Playing with your dog helps her to learn, to burn energy and to establish good manners, all of which help you to maintain control. Here are a few tips regarding play:

- Playing fetch with your dog is great exercise, particularly if you encourage your dog to run and catch an object such as a Frisbee. Try inventing different games or make a little assault course to keep your dog active while also challenging her brain.

- Teaching your dog to 'drop' an object during a fetch game is important because it establishes your command. Dogs will readily adhere to this when they realise that dropping the object is the only way play can continue. Reward such good behaviour with a treat in the early stages of learning to play safely.

- Do not try to wrestle an object from the jaws of your dog apart from in extreme circumstances. It is important that your dog doesn't become possessive over items because this can cause aggression.

- On a similar theme, tug toys are popular for puppies and older dogs. They can be fun, but it is best not to start a real tug of war with your dog because it can quickly develop into a competition of strength. While this is not a problem as a puppy, it could become more serious as your dog grows and matures. Simply stand your ground and allow the dog to pull. The game should stop when you say so and the dog should release the toy, then you may reward your dog for good behaviour. If at any time your dog begins to show signs of aggression, stop the game immediately and continue to teach your dog to play without hostility.

USING A LEAD

It is always advisable to use a lead when in a public area, no matter how well trained your dog. Think of it as a kind of insurance – something unexpected can always happen and your dog might suddenly give chase to an animal, or something could frighten her and cause her to bolt.

We never use choke chains on our dogs as there are plenty of good leads available that will help you to safely keep your dog in check on walks.

- The 'Halti Headcollar' is a well-known brand and it works along the same principle of a horse's head collar. It allows you to guide your dog gently and stops your dog pulling, to give you better control when out walking.
- The 'Gentle Leader Headcollar' uses the same concept of allowing you to lead your dog by the nose. The harness applies gentle pressure to the back of the neck and to the nose, which helps to inspire a naturally relaxed response.
- Once you feel your dog is well trained and will walk at your heel rather than pulling, you can switch to a more conventional lead.

You can train your puppy to walk on a lead from a young age and it is always helpful to establish good habits nice and early. Keep your puppy on a short lead and if she starts to pull simply stop walking altogether and tell your puppy to sit. Begin walking again, using your key word instruction, which could be 'heel' or 'walk' or whatever you like, and stop whenever your puppy starts to pull at the lead. Once your puppy has recognised that she is not allowed to try and drag you along you can reward her with a treat and her good habit will be reinforced.

If you want to be in the position of allowing your dog to wander without a lead when you are in a public place, you must be absolutely sure of her obedience and that she will come when you call .

You can practise the process of calling your dog at home in the garden or if you do not have a garden, try using an extending lead. Call your dog back whenever you like, at irregular intervals, and reward her for returning – at first with a treat and gradually with praise. Do not only call her when it is time to leave because after a while she may associate the call with leaving and choose to ignore you!

CAUSES OF AGGRESSION

There are many reasons why a dog may act aggressively.

- A dog may be hostile towards other dogs because she feels she is protecting her owner, or simply out of fear of the unknown. If a puppy is not socialised properly with older dogs as well as other puppies then this can lead to fear and aggression later in life.
- Your puppy may have had a nasty experience as a young dog, such as being attacked by another dog.
- Dogs are well known for chasing after postmen and milkmen and suchlike, and in these cases they are attempting to defend the home. Because these people always leave, dogs experience the feeling that they have succeeded by using aggression. They feel relieved and will continue that action in the future.
- If a puppy is brought up by an owner not obviously in control, the puppy may see itself as pack leader. This causes problems as the dog becomes older and larger and feels the need to protect the family.
- Dogs can be aggressive, both to humans and other dogs, when it comes to meals. This is because they grew used to acting this way when competing for food with brothers and sisters as a puppy.

CALMING AGGRESSION

Dealing with these moments of aggression depends on why your dog is acting in such a way:

- Proper socialisation with other dogs and humans from a young age helps a dog become confident with strangers and less likely to feel threatened.
- If your dog becomes cowed when out walking and is clearly wary of other dogs, make sure that you are the centre of attention so that your dog may play without

anxiety. The best way to do this is to divert them using a toy or a game.

- If your dog is frightened of or aggressive towards other dogs even in later life, you can carefully introduce her to new canine friends in a controlled atmosphere to help calm her emotions.

- Neutering significantly reduces the desire to be dominant in male dogs.

- More often than not your dog will be aggressive because of fear. Try to calm her and reward her when she reacts positively to strangers or new environments.

- From an early age, ensure you are in control at meal times. Do not allow your dog to bully you as you feed her. Train her to sit first and only when she is calm and behaving properly should you place the bowl down.

- Many people experience problems because of a lack of ground rules in the home. For example, if you allow your dog to sit on a settee then it psychologically raises their status. Think twice before you allow your dog to sit on the bed or the settee – keep yourself as the master in the relationship.

Specific Problems

Barking: Dogs bark when they are excited, as a warning to you and the family, out of fear and to ward off perceived threats, or in an effort to obtain attention from you. It is natural for dogs to bark, but there are limits.

- One way to limit barking, which we used with Gin, is to teach your dog to speak. Use a command, such as 'speak' and then praise and reward your dog for success. This helps your dog distinguish between barking and being quiet. When your dog heeds a command to stop barking, offer more praise.

- If your dog barks when the house is empty, try to distract her with a toy that will keep her amused, or remove the lonesome feeling your dog experiences when the front door closes by opening and closing it

occasionally without actually leaving the house.

- As mentioned earlier, shouting at your dog will not improve matters, indeed, it can make your dog bark even louder. This is about training your dog over a period of time, not shouting and hoping for the best.

Biting: Puppies in particular often bite during play and it can be quite painful, though they do not mean any harm.

- If your puppy does give you a nip, make plenty of fuss, even if it doesn't hurt, so that it recognises the error.
- Praise your dog for playing gently, but if you are bitten simply stop the game. This is punishment enough and your dog will soon understand what is not acceptable.
- Puppies often chew to soothe the pain of new teeth coming through, so make sure you have a chew toy handy – rather than your fingers!

Jumping: This can be a particularly annoying habit of dogs and very off-putting for guests in your home.

- The simplest way to deal with this is to ignore your dog when you come home. Ask visitors and other members of the family to do the same. Eventually, your dog will calm down, at which point you can offer a reward. Behaviour will soon alter once your dog realises that this undesirable behaviour yields no results.
- Alternatively, simply lowering yourself to your dog's level immediately negates the reason for jumping in the first place. Or, as above, refuse to make any fuss until your dog heeds your command to sit.

GINFORMATION!

- *Mental and physical stimulation – plenty of play – is the key to a happy, well-behaved dog. I'm always ready to fall asleep every evening because of the fun I've been having all day!*
- *Experiment with different games to see just how smart or agile we can be!*

Chapter Two

GETTING STARTED

How Dogs Learn

Dogs learn from a variety of sources and in a number of ways but it is perhaps most important to realise that dogs *enjoy* learning. It keeps them active both in mind and body and it is an opportunity for them to interact with you and receive your undivided attention. Also, learning inevitably involves rewards, whether that's affection or treats, which every dog loves!

LEARNING THROUGH PLAY

- It is always beneficial if your dog is having fun while learning. A dog has to learn to play and once it has grasped that play is a happy experience you can take that a step further and incorporate it into the training. Ensure your dog knows what is and isn't allowed during play – in other words, no biting or snatching.
- Always be careful to make it clear that there is a reason for the game. You are trying to teach a lesson, so don't allow yourself to be distracted from the real purpose.
- Teaching your dog to play and to interact with you and others has the long-term benefit of creating that special bond between you and your dog, as well as the advantages of owning a well-trained pet.

REPETITION

Repetition is one of the key ways a dog learns. By constantly praising and rewarding the completion of a particular activity, your dog will eventually begin to perform tasks naturally and purely for the pleasure of doing them right.

Let's take house-training as an example of how to teach your dog to learn.

- Choose an area in the garden where you want your new dog to relieve itself. Once your puppy urinates for the first time there (it's a good idea to place the puppy there after a meal, for example), give him plenty of love and attention and make a real fuss.

- Now for the repetition. Continue to take your puppy to that area when he is most likely to want to relieve himself. Good times are first thing in the morning, straight after meals and last thing at night. This repetition focuses on a routine that is followed by plenty of praise and will eventually harden in your puppy's mind.

- As part of your dog's training, establish a command that means your dog should relieve itself. My personal one is 'busy busy', but you can use any word or short phrase that you like. It is probably best to keep it neutral, though, for occasions when you're out in public! Again, your dog will begin to understand through repetition how he or she is expected to behave.

- In order to praise your dog for relieving itself in the right place, you need to be with your dog. So even if the weather is bad you'll have to be out there keeping him or her company while they do their business. Sending your dog out alone will only cause confusion.

- In time, your dog may well signal to you that he or she needs to go outside – this is a good step forward and a sign that the repetition has been working. Make sure you make plenty of fuss over your dog for that success.

- Your dog will not pick up all of this immediately and it will take a few months of persistence. However, when there are the inevitable mistakes by your dog it is imperative to refrain from scolding him or her. Always remember that your dog believes that to urinate or defecate wherever it likes is perfectly natural. You are working to change a completely understandable instinct. Telling your dog off for something it doesn't understand will achieve nothing, but praising your dog for doing something correctly reinforces the learning process.

REWARDS

Your dog will love receiving treats or being made a fuss over, which helps to instil the habit that you are trying to teach.

- The first time your dog sits correctly on your command you might reward him or her with a titbit or a lot of praise. Your dog will begin to associate his action with the reward and act accordingly.
- Different dogs respond to different rewards (see Rewards on p 66). Some prefer food but for others it can be more of a mental pleasure. For example, Gin clearly reacts positively to being able to perform a trick or a routine correctly, even if she doesn't get a treat.

YOUR ATTITUDE

Patience is really a virtue here. Dogs are not stupid animals and treating them as such will only result in behavioural problems. Here are some points to remember:

- Bellowing your disgust or even smacking your dog has no benefit whatsoever. You may feel better for getting it off your chest, but there will be consequences. Your dog may become confused, even aggressive, and these traits may manifest more severely later in life.
- Do not pander too much to your dog. If he or she is refusing to take part in your training and becomes wrapped up in an irrelevant game, do not encourage your dog by chasing it or otherwise being drawn in. Your dog is looking for attention. He or she enjoys that attention, so simply deny it. Don't get angry and shout, just ignore your dog, even walk away. Your dog will soon learn that the naughty behaviour is unacceptable and when he or she does calm down and obey you can offer a reward.
- While it is vital not to be nasty, don't be too nice either! Rewarding your dog before a task has been completed will be counter-productive and will not offer the best encouragement to your dog, who is merely learning that the bare minimum can bring a treat. In so doing your puppy can start to rule you and not vice-versa.

SOCIALISATION

As well as learning from their owners and other humans, dogs learn behaviour from other dogs. Socialisation, particularly at a young age, will encourage your puppy to be more confident and therefore less aggressive as he or she matures. From just six weeks old, Gin was learning to deal with our family and our other pets.

- It is not just the family that your puppy should meet. Once the vaccination process has been completed, he or she should meet as many different people as possible. Your dog will learn not to be over-protective or scared, and so aggressive, when seeing new faces.

- Socialisation classes are great places to meet other puppies, older dogs and humans. The puppies learn from each other how to play and how to act around humans. I took Gin to socialisation classes and although she was a bit of a terror it really helped her behaviour.

- Your dog may still be nervous around unfamiliar sounds or loud noises. Introduce such noises or bangs (music, the doorbell, washing machine and so forth) to your dog but be there to reassure him or her.

GINFORMATION!

- *Playing with a ball and learning to fetch and return is great exercise and also a valuable learning tool.*
- *Choose a socialisation class carefully. To make sure you pick one that suits you and your puppy, go along and watch one or two classes by yourself and form your own opinion about the instructors and the nature of the class.*
- *Keep your puppy lessons short and sharp. If they go on for too long, puppies will easily become bored!*

Understanding Dog Body Language

Dogs are constantly communicating their feelings and emotions and if you know what to look for then it is relatively easy to interpret them. They express numerous signals and while some are instantly recognisable, such as a wagging tail showing happiness, others are more subtle and it may take some practice to understand them fully.

Thanks to the special bond Gin and I have established over many years, it is relatively easy for me to understand how she's feeling. When her ears prick up and her tail wags, I know she's happy, but if her ears lean back I know she's showing concern. Sometimes I can even detect a general downcast look about her and she won't meet my gaze.

In the lead-up to the *Britain's Got Talent* semifinal Gin was becoming a little tired. I think she was feeling the pressure, plus we had to do many rehearsals and there was a problem with the flooring. Although she wanted to continue and she was happy as long as I was there, she just looked a little reserved. The signs at times such as these are pretty obvious, in this case because in general I was feeling the same as her!

This section will act as a guide to help you understand how your dog communicates.

THE EYES

- Dogs use their eyes to communicate, often to indicate superiority or submission.
- A dominant dog will hold a stare against a smaller or submissive dog to demonstrate superiority, while the other dog will look away.

● Unfortunately, the action of staring is not always easy to interpret. Dogs can and will stare at their owners, for example, but do so out of calm devotion.

● Equally, a dog may stare as a precursor to aggression if it feels threatened by a human, particularly a stranger.

● If a staring contest between two dogs escalates, one or both dogs may blink to calm things down. The blink breaks a stare interpreted as aggression. The more a dog blinks, the more contented the dog is feeling.

● A relaxed look in a dog's eyes is easy to spot. Their eyelids may droop and it is simple to notice the difference between that look and the alert gaze that occurs perhaps during play or when a dog feels unsure of a noise or event.

● Other looks echo those of humans – a wide-eyed look may mean fear, and you may come to recognise your dog averting her gaze when feeling bashful.

THE EARS

● The ears of a dog jolt to attention and move slightly forward when hearing a sound or expressing alertness. Obviously, this is more relevant to some breeds than others – a Spaniel or a Basset Hound do not have the same mobility in their long floppy ears compared with a Border Collie or an Alsatian.

● A combination of pricked up ears and a wagging tail is a sure sign of contentedness.

● I can often tell that Gin is unhappy, perhaps even remorseful, if her ears slant backwards, which is a common movement of the ears for dogs who are expressing an obedient or compliant attitude.

THE NOSE

Admittedly, you can't read anything from the nose itself, but scent plays an important role in communication for dogs, and they react strongly to scents and smells.

- You'll notice when out with your dog that she will always be sniffing, nose towards the ground, searching out different scents. Watch carefully and you may even be able to tell from your dog's reactions what scent they have picked up - if your dog suddenly seems cowed she may have detected the smell of a more dominant dog that has been in the area.

- Related to this is your dog's keenness to mark their territory by urinating or perhaps scratching at the ground when you're out walking. It serves as a warning to other dogs and also overpowers the existing scent of other dogs.

- Your dog's own scent is important because of the rich information it holds for other dogs regarding individual personality and strength - dogs often circle each other before performing a sniffing ritual to gather this kind of data. For this reason not all dogs enjoy bath time!

THE FACE

- Once again, it is helpful to imagine the expressions on the human faces that we interpret every day. A human concentrating strongly on a task might furrow a brow or display other obvious signals of tension. It is the same with a dog - when skin appears to tighten around the face, particularly at the forehead, it is a sign that your dog is attentive. By the same token, as your dog relaxes, so do the muscles and skin around your dog's face.

- Other signs are extremely obvious – showing teeth and snarling is a clear indicator of aggression. Yet a similar movement of the lips can also denote obedience or humility in anticipation of being told off for doing something your dog knows is wrong. Dad has a Labrador that often shifts his lips to the side in this manner and it really looks as if he is smiling.
- You'll most often observe the tongue when your dog is feeling content and happy in your company, but also if your dog is hot, exhausted or upset in some way. Panting helps to relieve stress by lowering a dog's temperature.
- Dogs sometimes yawn because it helps them to feel less stressed.

THE TAIL

- I think it is safe to say that we all know that a wagging tail means a dog is feeling happy, pleased or delighted. You'll often see this as a gesture of anticipation before an event your dog loves, such as eating or playing or going for a walk. Some dogs even manage to shake their whole body in excitement! Dogs also like to lie down and wag their tail as an overt invitation to be stroked or patted.
- A wagging tail can also mean a dog is angry, particularly if the tail is tense and swishes strongly.
- Another way of recognising tension or anxiety in your dog is if the tail is rigid and almost horizontal.
- Everyone has heard the term of someone retreating 'with their tail between their legs'. It is a good metaphor, because dogs do exactly this after a confrontation in which they have been forced to back down.

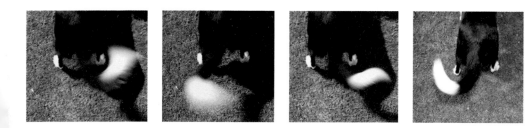

Posture

- You may notice your dog waiting patiently by resting her head between her paws while you concentrate on something else. This is a submissive posture that shows good obedience.
- All dogs love to play and many have a particularly recognisable bowing posture that tells you they want to have some fun. Their hindquarters will point up and their front paws will be flat in front, demonstrating that they are ready for action!
- Another indication of a desire to play, particularly with puppies, is the act of chasing their own tail.
- A dog lying on its stomach with paws stretched in front is calm yet simultaneously alert.
- If the dog's legs are to the side it is more relaxed, perhaps ready to doze off.

Sounds

- The most obvious of all dog sounds is of course the bark, which can be used to attract attention, as a warning, as a note of pleasure or as a threat.
- If a dog uses a higher pitch, it is excited or pleased.
- It is quite typical for dogs to bark at strangers venturing towards the home. This is both a sound of warning to you and a note of aggression towards what they perceive to be a threat. This bark will be lower, and more guttural, to give the impression of a large dog.
- A dog may also bark when in distress or because of a feeling of boredom or frustration.
- The growl of a dog is always a sign of displeasure or hostility. The dog may be hurt and therefore afraid and wary of being touched. A dog may feel threatened by other dogs and, especially if on a lead, can feel

cornered, so the growl acts as a defence mechanism. The growl will intensify if the initial warning is not heeded and you'll also notice that telltale sign of lips curling and teeth showing.

- Just as a lighter bark indicates happiness, so a whine is a much more compliant sound than the growl. It can indicate a wide range of things, but it is basically an attempt to attract attention, perhaps hoping for food or loving care, or to denote a feeling of discomfort.
- If a dog is retreating from a confrontation, a whimper will often accompany the tail between the legs.

SIGNS OF AFFECTION

- Dogs love to be patted and stroked by those that they trust – it helps to make them feel relaxed and secure, perhaps because it reminds them of the camaraderie they shared with their brothers and sisters as puppies. However, if a dog backs away as you go to stroke it, do not persist, as the dog feels threatened. Let it come to you and gain your scent and feel comfortable first.
- Your dog may reciprocate your stroking by licking your hands or even your face as a gesture of pleasure. Licking can also act as a kind of apology after being told off.
- If your dog rolls over to have its tummy tickled, it is a sure sign your dog feels secure and confident with you and is in a state of total relaxation.

GINFORMATION!

- *There are many signs that will indicate that your dog might be feeling under the weather: A lack of appetite, a bored or lethargic appearance, or if she scoots along the floor on her backside. There are more obvious signs, such as vomiting or leakages from the eyes or nose.*
- *Some older bitches occasionally experience phantom pregnancies where they will act as if they are about to give birth and will even treat some toys as if they were their pups!*

Basic Training
'sit'

This is usually the first command for your dog to learn after he knows his name. This action is also the easiest to teach, because your dog will naturally go into the sitting position when he is feeling expectant.

2 Move your hand slowly and steadily over his head. The dog will move his nose upwards, following the treat, which will make his rear end move downwards towards the floor. As he reaches the sitting position, say 'sit' firmly and clearly.

1 Begin by getting your dog's full attention. Get your dog to look at you, if necessary by saying his name, and then wait a moment. Hold a small morsel of food in front of your dog's nose so that he can smell it.

4 Once you have achieved this, hold the food behind your back in your left hand and use your right hand to guide the dog into a sitting position by raising it slightly over his head, as if still holding the food, and say 'sit'. When he sits, reward him.

3 Give him his treat and tell him how good he is. After repeating this several times he will start to sit as soon as you hold the morsel of food in your hand.

'stay'

This simple task is essential for a well-behaved dog. Your dog should stay in one place whatever the distractions or attractions – even a cat!

2 Place your right hand, palm open right, near to your dog's nose and clearly say the word 'Stay'.

1 Stand still with your dog sitting or standing just behind you. Hold a treat in your left hand so that he can see it.

3 Praise your dog and after 1 to 2 seconds let him come to you, then give him some treats. Always reward even the slightest understanding.

4 Move away further and increase the amount of time your dog remains in the stay position.

'come'

An important command to learn at the beginning is the command to 'come'. It is a good idea, though not essential, to begin to teach this command with a long lead. An extendable lead is ideal; otherwise you can attach a longer cord to your ordinary lead.

1 Tell your dog to 'sit' then back away a few paces. Call out 'come' emphatically. If he seems hesitant, call him again with the cue word, 'come' (give a little tug on the lead if using one).

2 When he comes, give him lots of praise and a treat. If using a lead, when he has come to you several times, you can take it off. This time you can add a sign. If he does not come, don't punish him. He should not be afraid to come to you

3 Praise your dog once he has come to you and reinforce your praise with a titbit or toy. If, when you are out in the garden or park and he is off the lead and will not come to you when you give the command, a good ploy is to walk away from him. Dogs will usually run after you, as they won't want to be left behind.

'Flat'

The down position is a little harder to teach, but persevere, as it is an important command for your dog to understand. By getting him to drop to the floor in a flat position, you can get him to avoid possible danger and make him less threatening to people who are nervous of dogs. Decide whether you want to use the cue word 'flat' or 'down', bearing in mind that you may shout 'down' at him at other times in his life, without meaning this particular position!

1 Begin with your dog in his sitting position. Show him the treat to get his attention. Now close the treat in your hand with your fingers pointing downward and move your closed hand from the front of his nose slowly down towards the floor.

2 Keep your hand close to him or he may walk forwards. Your dog will ease downwards into a crouching position. You can then give him the treat, but don't say 'flat' unless he is right down on the floor in the position you want him to get into.

3 Keep repeating the exercise, getting him to drop lower and lower. You can keep your closed hand on the floor so that he snuffles around it searching for the food. This will encourage him to drop lower into the correct flat position. When he reaches the right position, say the cue word, 'flat', and reward him with the treat.

4 Next you can dispense with the treat and instead use your hand to make a downwards sign. Try pointing your finger and lowering it slowly from above his head towards the floor, so that you end up by pointing to the floor as you say 'flat'. Make a fuss of him and give him his treat when he has been successful at this exercise.

GINFORMATION!

- Don't repeat his name every time you give him a command.
- You can use any words you like to train your dog. Think of words that sound different from each other. Only use a particular word for one action.
- Give clear hand signs. Use the same words with the same hand signs each time. Be consistent.
- Write your signs and words down and pin the list somewhere your family can see. Never let anyone give your dog commands if they don't follow your 'cue' words and signs.
- Have rewards handy.

Chapter Three
TRICKS & TRAINING

LEARNING TO TRAIN GIN

From the moment I first marvelled at the dog competitions at Crufts I dreamed of training my own Border Collie. To see those dogs perform their jumps and twists, almost like four-legged dancers, was amazing. The idea of training a dog to reach that level was an inspiration and I couldn't wait to get started. Yet I knew I had to be realistic. It was going to take a lot of hard work, patience and perseverance.

Perhaps the most important factor to take into consideration was to make sure that Gin was ready both in mind and body before starting my programme. A dog must be at least 12 months old before their joints, particularly their shoulders and their knees, are strong enough to cope with the pressure and strain of a lot of jumping and sharp movements. If I had been impatient and started before Gin was a year old, I could have damaged her body.

Because Gin was so lively, she had to possess a basic grounding in obedience before we could move on to the more fun aspect of learning the fantastic tricks she can perform today. It would be pointless during a competition if, having achieved one particular manoeuvre flaw- lessly, Gin turned and bolted straight out of the arena! I had to learn how to harness Gin's natural energy through plenty of play, especially in the early days.

Despite Gin's endearing hyperactive nature, I soon noticed that she was particularly clever. She took to each new trick extraordinarily quickly. Sometimes it was almost scary, as if she instinctively knew what to do, and the more I taught her the better she became at learning. She simply excelled at everything.

After we appeared on *Britain's Got Talent* quite a few people approached me, remembering the crazy, young Gin, the dog that always had to do everything at 100 miles per hour, and how at the obedience classes she would run round and round my legs, barking and squealing. They were surprised that I had persisted with a mad dog like Gin, but in fact I had never even considered giving up on her. I could see how intelligent she was and I persevered. I always knew what she could achieve in the end.

Gin loved to be taught new tricks, perhaps because it felt like a wonderful game for her, and as she matured her adaptability and ability to learn only improved. Yet it is vital to remember that the foundation of all Gin's exciting capabilities is basic obedience.

Let's take an example of the importance of obedience. If you are taking part in a competition and your dog fouls in the ring, you are immediately eliminated. It doesn't matter if your dog performs a superb routine that has the audience cheering wildly, everything will be wasted if good old Rover then urinates as he leaves the ring. Reaching that level of control and obedience takes hard work, persistence and patience, but it has been fantastic to work with Gin. These days, Gin is so perfectly house-trained that she actually pees on my command, which is especially useful in competitions. And, if you want to know, my special command for Gin on these occasions is: 'Busy Busy!'

The best thing about training is
without doubt the delicious treats.
They smell so nice and savoury that
I could follow that lovely gravy smell
through Kate's legs a thousand times and
more if it was necessary. She taught
me to bow by putting a treat on the
floor and to crawl along on my belly after a
titbit. She also taught me to follow her stick with my
eyes and when she lifts it up, to jump over it. She is so
enthusiastic about my triumphs, small and large, from
a dutiful busy, busy pee to when I jump into her arms
when we have completed our routine. Her smiling face
is what I'm looking for, but I have to say that the treats in
her pocket are what I think about quite a lot too.

Timetables for Training

Start training your puppy immediately, because when they're little they pick up more. You're like their mum, and they naturally learn from their mum. They'll follow your behaviour when they are young.

GETTING STARTED

You should aim to have your puppy trained in the basic commands using your words and signs by the time he's six months. Anything that has an impact on his joints, like agility training and advanced tricks, should come later, after he is 12 months old. You should also avoid excessive walking until your puppy is mature. Bigger breeds mature more slowly than small breeds. You can check with the breeder, or a book about the breed, exactly how long it will take for your puppy to be fully grown.

It is best to start with short, interesting training sessions every day, or even several times a day. Training sessions should last no longer than ten minutes for a puppy. Adult dogs can cope with 20-minute sessions. If you try and teach your dog for long periods of time he may become bored. However, as your dog gets older and becomes used to learning, he will probably be happy to spend longer with you in a training session. If you have a very energetic dog that finds it hard to focus, it may be a good idea to take him for a walk or play vigorously with him before the session.

If a person is taught to perform a task in one place, they will generally be able to repeat the same task in a different location. This ability is called 'generalizing behaviour'. Dogs are not people and they will not be able to repeat their commands and tricks in different locations without retraining from you. Each breed and each individual dog will also have different generalizing abilities. Therefore, be prepared to go through the basic training for each command or trick in different places to enable your dog to generalize. Try teaching him the same thing inside the house, in the garden and then in the park, at a friend's house and on a quiet street.

Professional trainers calculate that it takes about six weeks to train an adult dog in basic behaviours and commands. But every dog is an individual with a different personality, and each one will be a different 'type' according to his breed. You should be able to train your puppy in about four weeks to perform the basic commands. You can then take longer to go through as many of the tricks shown in this book as you would like to.

PREPARATION IS IMPORTANT

- Remember to have a selection of treats available for your dog...
- ...but only give your dog the treat when he is in the correct position!
- Get any props that you might need ready first.
- Begin by teaching each new command on the lead.
- Take the lead off when you know that your dog is concentrating.

MAKING A TIMETABLE

To help you and your puppy learn it is useful to create a timetable, mapping out your targets and the time needed for training commands and tricks. Remember to consolidate each new exercise before you move on. If you or your dog is having a problem, simply go back to the beginning of the exercise and start again. Practise makes perfect! The timetable we have shown here is only a guide. You can vary it to fit in with you and your lifestyle, and to suit your dog and his personality.

Basic Commands with Words and Signs

WEEK ONE: Using his name and the command 'Come' (see pp 52–53). For the first few days simply practise using your puppy's name so that he gets used to it. Call his name clearly with enthusiasm to make him look at you and then praise him. Don't keep repeating his name, he will ignore it if he hears it a lot.

On the third day attach a long lead to his collar and go through the technique shown for calling him to you with the command 'Come'. In later sessions try this without the lead.

WEEK TWO: The commands 'Sit' (see pp 48–49) and 'Flat' (see pp 54–55). Practise the word and sign for 'Sit' for two days and then, if he has mastered that, go on to practise the command for 'Flat' for the next two days. On the following day practise doing both commands in a sequence.

WEEK THREE: Practise all three commands. Spend ten minutes once or twice a day going through all three commands. If you have been practising these in the house, now is the time to try them out in the garden.

WEEK FOUR: Consolidating and generalizing. Your dog should be listening to you and be confident in all three commands. Now you can take him to other locations where you can retrain him to understand the commands in new places. Keep him on the lead to keep him safe.

Simple Tricks

WEEK ONE: 'Bow' (see pp 82–83) and 'Roll over' (see pp 98–99). This week start with training your dog to do a 'Bow'. After another day of practising this you can add the 'Roll over'. This move can be quite tricky so persevere.

WEEK TWO: 'Spin' (see pp 84–85) and 'Beg' (see pp 102–103). Start the week by practising the 'Bow' and the 'Roll over'. The next day you can train him to do a 'Spin'. Consolidate 'Spin' the following day. At the end of the week you can go through the sequence to teach him to 'Beg.'

WEEK THREE: Consolidating and generalizing. Repeat all four of the above moves at home. When you feel he is confident in any or all of them you can take him to some different locations and retrain him there.

WEEK FOUR: 'High' (see pp 86–87) **and 'Crawl'** (see pp 108–109). Take two days to teach him 'High' and then spend the next two days going over 'Crawl' with him. If he seems to understand both moves try them together the next day.

WEEK FIVE: Practice and improving. Practise the tricks that he can do well in different locations. Work on any that need improving at home in a calm environment.

Specific Tricks

WEEK ONE: Brain training – 'Leave and take' (see pp 128–129). On the first day of the week go through the sequence to teach him to 'leave' and 'take'. Spend the next day practising this in different positions and places. **Target training – 'Touch'** (see pp 120–121). In the middle of the week begin to teach him to 'Touch' using a stick. **Simple Tricks for Exercise and Fun – 'Walk back'** (see pp 88–89). Add an agility skill at the end of the week with a 'Walk back'.

WEEK TWO: Brain Training – 'Find' (see pp 118–119). Begin the week with the fun game of 'find'. **Target training – 'Touch'** (see pp 120–121). Continue this training by teaching your dog to touch the stick without there being a lure on the end. **– 'Walk backwards through legs'** (see pp 106–107). Teach the skill of a 'Walk through' at the end of the week.

WEEK THREE: Consolidate. Consolidate all the above tricks, combining different training skills in one day. Try to take the 'Touch' trick a stage further by encouraging him to touch your hand or an object that you hold out to him.

WEEK FOUR: 'Jumping over a stick' (see pp 104–105). Start the week by teaching him to 'jump over'. If he has this trick by the second day, keep practising and on the following day practise all the tricks he has learnt so far in the sequence of Advanced Tricks (see **pp 96-109**). When he is ready, take him to different locations to retrain him.

WEEK FIVE: 'Put away' (see pp 130–131). You can devote this week to teaching him the Brain Training skill of putting his toys away, which needs to be taught in stages.

- Begin the week by getting him to retrieve a toy for you and then learning to 'drop' it on command.
- When he has that part of the trick you can add the next bit, which is to get him to 'drop' his toy into the basket.
- Once he has the entire trick, then you can ask him to pick up more than one toy in each session.
- Your aim is to get him to retrieve several toys and drop them in the basket after you call 'Put away!'

Flyball

This is something that you'll have to join a club to learn and compete in properly. But if your dog can already jump and retrieve for you, then you have given him a head start in learning how to play the game (see **pp 76-77**).

GINFORMATION!

- *The timetables above are only a guide. Make up your own timetables to suit you and your dog.*
- *Be realistic.*
- *Don't worry if your dog takes longer to learn something than you had anticipated.*
- *Keep consolidating, even when your dog is confident.*
- *Pin your timetable somewhere you can see it easily. Tick off tricks as you and your dog achieve them. This is motivating!*
- *Repeat his training in different locations.*
- *Don't go through with a session if you or your dog are having an 'off' day.*
- *Practise makes perfect!*

Rewards

The secret to persuading your dog to act the way you would like is partly down to treats and rewards. A dog is appreciative of treats in whatever form and will respond positively to this kind of treatment. Like all dogs, Gin loves food as treats, but having said that, she is also absolutely mad about balls. Giving her a ball to chase around for a while is therefore just as effective as food in rewarding good behaviour.

When dishing out a tasty treat it's important to remember to offer it immediately after your dog has acted correctly or performed a task successfully. This ensures that your dog understands exactly why she is receiving the reward. If you wait even for a few seconds your dog will not link the two events in her mind and an opportunity will have been lost.

EDIBLE TREATS

There are a variety of edible treats you can give your dog to show her how pleased you are with her actions, which encourages her to repeat this good deed in the future. With all of these treats it is advisable to use them only in moderation and always check the ingredients of any treat you decide to buy for any unwanted additives.

Doggy Treats: You can choose from a wide selection of dried food treats, dog chocolate treats or dog biscuit treats from supermarkets or pet shops. They work well and can be quite nutritious. However, if you are like us and own a few dogs, this can become a little expensive, so you may like to explore other options.

Sausage: It can be more economical to buy sausage treats for your dog. Gin loves sausage, so I often use this when we are training. You can cut them up into smaller pieces for miniature treats if you like.

Cheese: We often buy large blocks of the cheaper cheeses and cut them into small, bite-size squares. All our dogs love cheese as a treat, so it works well and is economical too. Don't overdo the cheese, though! Keep the treats nice and small so your dog feels rewarded without eating too much. In some cases, eating cheese can result in hyperactivity in a dog.

Liver: Gin is a big fan of liver. You can purchase some from the butcher's and cut it up into small pieces. Alternatively, there are various methods of cooking your own liver treats to make the meat go a little further, using flour and eggs and baking in the oven. There are plenty of great recipes online if you fancy this route! You can also buy special liver tablets if you prefer.

GINFORMATION!

- Be very careful when feeding your dog! Although we like chocolate treats made especially for us, we cannot eat real chocolate as it makes us sick. It can cause liver damage and can be fatal.
- I love treats, but don't spoil your dog's appetite with too many!
- As your dog begins to learn how to behave, gradually remove edible treats and replace them with praise and maybe a cuddle!

Balls and Games

Part of training your dog is teaching her how to play properly and without aggression. The most common game is fetch with a ball, Frisbee or even a soft toy. When you are training your puppy you can encourage this game by making a fuss of her whenever she retrieves the object and particularly when she drops it for you. In return you can then throw the object again so the game can carry on. This way, your dog will be rewarded for good behaviour and for playing safely because the game is continuing. In effect, the game becomes the reward because your dog is having a great time playing with you and exercising at the same time.

Through playing with toys your dog will learn how to gain rewards. You'll teach her not to snap at a toy when you are holding it, not to bite you under any circumstances, to drop a toy at your command and to return to you upon your call. All of these lessons will lead to safe, healthy play that both you and your dog can enjoy.

Toy Tips

Be careful to choose toys that are suitable for your dog.

Balls: Ensure any ball you give your dog cannot be swallowed as this can obviously result in great difficulties for your dog. If you own a cat, make sure their small toys are kept away from your dog. Tennis balls are particularly good for playing fetch. Some dogs love to play with a full-sized football, dribbling it around the park or a garden with their nose.

Frisbees: Suitable for most dogs and fantastic exercise for energetic dogs. To thoroughly master the game they have to run, jump, twist and return so it really gives them a thorough workout!

Rubber toys and Squeakers: Many dogs enjoy these. Our Welsh Terriers particularly love toys that squeak and make a noise, I suppose because it makes them feel as if they are hunting, which is what they were bred for.

Kongs: These are shaped a little like hand grenades. They are made of rubber and hollowed out so that you place various treats inside.

Using a Clicker

In the past I have sometimes used a 'clicker' as part of Gin's training. It acts as a kind of reward and I found that she reacted quite well to this method. It is particularly effective for distance training.

- A clicker is a small plastic implement that you hold in your hand when you are training. When your dog performs a task successfully, you press the button to send out a clicking sound, which, through training, your dog will come to understand as a sound of approval.

- Obviously, your dog will not immediately recognise that the click is an indication of praise and approval. The first thing to do is to associate the sound with a treat by clicking and then feeding your dog a treat without her having to do anything first.

- The next step is to ask your dog to perform a task, such as to sit. Follow that with a click and then reinforce it with the offer of an edible treat.

- In this way, the clicker becomes linked in your dog's mind to an enjoyable reward and over time she will begin to understand the clicking as recognition of a job well done and a reward in itself.

- Gradually, you should remove the edible treat and

replace it with some encouraging words or a warm cuddle! This is advisable to ensure that your dog does not become conditioned to expecting a treat every time she hears the click.

- Dog owners use the clicker in different ways. While some simply click once to congratulate the dog, others prefer to increase the clicking to correspond with consistently good behaviour or training.
- A clicker is particularly helpful if more than one person is training a dog, because it is a method that does not rely solely on one particular voice.
- The advantage of the clicker is that if your dog is not by your side and you are unable to offer her a physical treat, you can still offer the reward of clicking and your dog will know she has behaved well or performed a task correctly. When your dog returns to your side you can offer a treat or words of praise. The hearing of a dog is so acute that they can hear the clicking from some distance.

Using a Whistle

- A dog whistle can be used in training in much the same way as a clicker.
- It is particularly effective if you live in the countryside and your dog may roam out of sight when you are out for a walk.
- It is a great tool to recall your dog and once she returns you can offer a treat or some love to show that you are pleased with her behaviour. In that way, your dog will realise that responding to a recall whistle will be worth their while.

Using Training Discs

These are not something I have felt the need to use with Gin, but they can be beneficial. The idea is opposite to that of a clicker. The noise of these discs jingled together tells your dog that a reward is not forthcoming and that behaviour has been bad. If you can teach your dog to understand that this sound means no reward, then you can start to eliminate undesirable behaviour.

- Use the discs in conjunction with your usual reward programme so that your dog can soon come to understand the difference.
- To begin this training process, reward your dog for performing a task correctly with a treat. Next, with your dog a few paces away and seated, place a treat in front of you. When she comes to get it, remove it and drop the discs instead.
- As you repeat this process, your dog will come to understand that the sound of the discs indicates that there will be no reward.
- Discs should only be used to correct persistently bad behaviour and should be used sparingly. Only address urgent problems first. Keep training sessions very short, just a few minutes, and always keep in mind that reward-based training is almost universally perceived as the most effective method and also the most enjoyable for you and your dog.

Agility

Once you have trained your dog to be an obedient companion, to be friendly with others and reliable in public, you may wish to take things a little further, like I did with Gin, and consider some more complicated training, perhaps with a view to entering competitions.

That was certainly my ambition from a young age. My older sister, Laura, trained one of our Welsh Terriers and actually performed in the main ring at Crufts with the Young Kennel Club. To reach that stage is some achievement, because Welsh Terriers are not exactly easy dogs to train in agility! Laura also enjoyed the grooming categories, but I loved the amazing tricks that dogs could be trained to perform. Border Collies are often the best in that category because of their intelligence and the enjoyment they receive out of being challenged in that manner, and that is why I was so keen on owning a dog like Gin.

You may like to start training your own dog in this way, but it is vital to ensure that your dog has grasped the basics of obedience first. If you do not have basic obedience from your dog, you have no hope of achieving anything more complicated!

Ensure that you research the breed of your dog fully. I could not start training with Gin until she was a year old, fully grown and with strong joints and muscles that could cope with the rigours of agility training. Different dogs mature at different ages, so make sure you don't start too early as your dog could get injured.

ARE YOU READY?

Training is certainly a great deal of fun,

but it is incredibly hard work. The routines that you may have seen Gin perform on television have taken years to establish and perfect. Even teaching a dog as quick and intelligent as Gin a trick such as walking backwards took months and months of slow progress.

The idea of having an intelligent dog who can dance, walk backwards and do clever jumps is appealing, but not everybody will have the time and patience to spend the hours, weeks and months needed to play with a dog and gradually build up a repertoire of tricks. It is up to you whether or not to move on to this next stage and how seriously you want to take it, but if you do, here are a few qualities you'll need:

- **Patience**. This is absolutely key to the process. If you are impatient and need to see immediate results, you are going to be very disappointed.
- **Consistency**. Consider what you want to teach and when. You could plan a timetable if that helps, but be deliberate in your methods and don't try to teach too many things at once. Choose one trick at a time and perfect it before moving on, otherwise your dog may become confused.
- **Enthusiasm**. If you begin to see this sort of training as a chore, it is probably not for you or your dog. If you enjoy it, so will your dog and if you are having fun then that is half the battle. Don't be disheartened if things take longer than you expected - persevere and your hard work will be rewarded.
- **Be dog-like**. It can help to try and put yourself in the mind of your dog! This sounds difficult but I think much of this sort of ability comes from the bond you build with your dog from the first time you meet - from feeding your dog, to playing, walking and learning together. You'll soon learn to recognise your dog's thoughts and feelings. A natural affinity with dogs certainly helps - Mum thinks I'm half dog because I seem to understand Gin so well!

Is Your Dog Ready?

Remember that not all dogs will take to learning tricks and routines readily. Working breeds such as Border Collies may love it, just as Gin does, but others may simply not possess the correct temperament.

- Larger dogs may not enjoy agility training. Remember that large breeds such as Labradors won't be mature enough in their bone structure until they are two or even three years old. That's not to say that larger breeds cannot be taught. I remember seeing a Great Dane doing agility at one competition, which was a pretty impressive sight! But smaller dogs, like Gin, are lighter as well as being strong, so it comes more naturally.
- At the other end of the spectrum, smaller dogs, such as toy breeds, are not really bred for such intensive exercise. They are companion dogs and do not even need a great deal of walking. They will probably be reluctant to learn complicated dance routines, no matter how good the music is!
- If you decide to get an older dog rather than a puppy, I do firmly believe you can still teach some of them tricks. You need to establish a relationship, of course, but if the dog is mobile and fit then there's no reason why you can't embark on a training programme. Old dogs can learn new tricks!

Naturally, you don't have to train your dog to the levels needed for competition. This sort of training is simply great fun for your dog, who will love the mental and physical stimulation being received, as well as the opportunity to spend some great play time with you.

When I began training Gin, she took to everything amazingly quickly. She picked up new tricks with relative ease, almost as if she had been born for it! You can play some games with your dog to see if she has the aptitude to go a little further. You could start by building a little obstacle course in the garden and working on the route together with your dog. Below are a few ideas of obstacles you could include, but use your imagination and test your dog's intelligence!

- Place a plank of wood across two upturned buckets. You can train your dog to walk the plank, jump over it, or crawl under it.
  - Using some rope, suspend an old tyre from a branch and encourage your dog to leap through – obviously this isn't advisable for particularly large dogs!
  - Use a couple of garden implements (gnomes, buckets, watering cans – anything will do) as goalposts and place a ball in the course for your dog to dribble. Encourage your dog to score a goal between the posts.
- You can buy play tunnels for dogs to crawl through, which are great fun.
- You can also buy kits that have the materials to set up a high jump, although you can easily make a high jump of your own using wood.
- Place a series of cones (or buckets) in a line and teach your dog to weave between them.

THE NEXT STAGE

Of course, all dogs are special, especially your own! However, if you believe that yours can go that extra stage further you may want to consider agility classes or competitions. Naturally **Crufts** is the ultimate goal. However, The Kennel Club now runs **Scruffts**, a fun competition especially for crossbreeds, with a final each year to find the Family Crossbreed Dog of the Year.

GINFORMATION!

- *The Agility Club is the largest club of its kind registered to the Kennel Club. Visit their website for more information about becoming a member and where to find an agility club near you: www.agilityclub.co.uk*
- *For more information about Scruffts, visit the Kennel Club website: www.thekennelclub.org.uk*
- *For more information about Crufts, visit their website: www.crufts.org.uk*

Flyball

This is a relay race for dogs and Gin loves this event. Gin and her team won the British Flyball Championship in 2007, so Flyball is definitely one of Gin's skills. Along with dancing of course!

There are usually six dogs in each team. There are five Collies and one crossbreed in Gin's team.

Flyball is an extremely exciting sport and is a great way of burning off the high energy levels that some dogs have. Although herding dogs, such as Border Collies, German Shepherds and nimble Terriers tend to dominate this sport, it is perfectly possible for all kinds of breeds to take part and enjoy it. It is quite common for many crossbreeds to show a real talent for Flyball.

Dogs gain titles and awards based on points earned by their team. The event works rather like a human relay race and the course is 15.5 metres long. The lanes have mesh on each side so that the competing dogs can run at the same time. Each lane has four hurdles in it and a Flyball box at the end, with balls in it. The hurdle height is determined by the shoulder height of the smallest dog in the team.

Each team will use four dogs for each race. When the whistle sounds, the teams release a dog out into their lane. The racing dog must leap over the four jumps before reaching the Flyball box. The box automatically shoots out a tennis ball to be caught

when the dog presses a spring-loaded pad. The dog must return over the same four hurdles while carrying the tennis ball in his mouth. As the first dog returns over the start/

finish line with the ball in his mouth, the next one can begin to run. The first team to get all four dogs home without dropping a ball is the winning team.

A dog must be agile and fast to compete. He must be able to jump and to retrieve.

If you are interested in Flyball racing, the Kennel Club Information Office will give you the name and address of the club nearest to you that handles Flyball. The British Flyball Association also has lists of teams and events.

GINFORMATION!

- Focus on Brain, Target and Agility Training.
- Put aside some time for each of these training specialities.
- Vary the treats you give your dog to keep him interested.
- Use props safely. It is vital to make sure there are no sharp edges or points.
- When he has a trick, try it out in a different environment.
- Try performing in front of someone.
- Take each new trick slowly.
- Don't forget your words and signs.
- Keep training sessions fun.
- Like the idea of Flyball? Go along to an event near you to watch.

Signs and Words

Patience is the most important thing when you're training your dog. Try and think like a dog! That's what I do. Start off with just five minutes a day. Gin and I work together every day, but we started just like this. Don't forget to reward your dog every time he gets it right.

WORDS

- It is up to you to decide which cue words you want to train your dog with.
- It is sensible, however, to choose words that are easy to remember and stick with the ones you've decided on.
- Try and use words that sound different from each other. For example, 'heel' and 'here' sound similar. It may be better to substitute 'come' for 'here'.
- Make sure all the family know and use the same words and signs so that your dog doesn't become confused.
- Be careful not to give your dog a cue word that you might inadvertently give at other times for another reason. For example, 'down' can be used for making your dog lie flat on the floor, but you may also want to say it when he jumps up at people. So, in that case you could use 'flat' to make your dog lie on the floor.
- Dogs may not understand words, but they do understand food! To begin with you will need to use a doggy treat to lure your dog into the right position in order to help him understand your command.
- To begin with say the cue word with the sign just after you lure your dog into obeying the command with the treat. Then reward him with the treat and lots of praise.

Repeat this until your dog begins to understand what the word 'sit' and the 'sit' sign means, and that if he performs the right action, he'll get a reward.

- The correct sequence is command, pause, action, reward.
- When you think your dog understands the cue word and the accompanying hand sign you can perform them without the treat. Eventually you can stop giving him treats every time and just say 'good boy'.

SIGNS

- To help your dog to understand what you want you can use hand and/or arm signs as well as the cue word.
- Make sure that your signs are clear and simple and that you stick to the same ones every time.
- Use the cue word and the sign together to reinforce each other and to help your dog know what you want.

NAME

Begin to teach your dog his cue words and signs in a quiet place where there are no distractions. Inside the house is a good place. Later, you can train him in different locations. The most important word your dog must learn is his name!

- Use his name to get his attention, and repeat it clearly till he responds. Then reward him.
- Call his name in an excited, positive voice. Ideally, your dog should look at you the first time you call his name. Then you can make a fuss of him and give him a treat.
- If he doesn't look at you the first time, don't keep repeating his name. Instead, clap your hands loudly to get his attention. If you keep saying his name it will become meaningless.
- When he looks at you, look back at him calmly, making eye contact. But don't stare, a glance is enough.
- Your aim should be that every time you say his name he looks up at you to see what you want.
- Once you have his attention you can introduce cue words to give him simple commands. Don't say his name every time you give him a command, otherwise the name and the cue word will merge together.

Simple Tricks for Exercise and Fun

Gin was such a naughty puppy! But the more I taught her, the better she got at learning. I wasn't going to give up. I was just going to keep training her. I am sure your dog will love learning new tricks, but try and keep them simple when you start.

Once your dog has mastered the simple commands of answering to his name, coming, sitting and lying down using your special words and signs, then you can move on to some simple tricks. This will provide your dog with exercises for his body and brain; and it will be lots of fun for you both. All types of dogs can do tricks, but certain breeds, like Collies, may find them easier.

Use the same technique as the one you have already mastered in the *Signs and Words* section (see pp 78-79). You'll be using different words and signs now, but the routine will be the same: use a treat to lure him into doing the trick, and then reward him and tell him what the trick is called. Use the same hand movements each time you do the trick so that your dog will not get confused.

Make a regular quiet time for you and your dog and spend ten minutes training him to do these tricks. Just tackle one trick at a time. But remember that dogs can sometimes be like humans and have an 'off' day when they don't concentrate. In which case, leave the training session for another day. These tricks will take longer for you and your dog to master than the basic commands, but with plenty of patience and practice you will be able to get your dog to perform these simple but impressive tricks.

Trick 1
BOW

In this trick your dog will perform a neat bow. When he performs this trick he'll wow everybody you meet with his good manners.

1 Use his name to get your dog to stand still. Show him the treat in your hand. Move your other hand towards his stomach.

2 Put the treat very close to his nose and begin to lower your hand so that he begins to bow his head. Place your other hand gently but firmly flat against his stomach to prevent his whole body from moving downwards.

3 Continue to move the treat towards the floor. Your dog should dip his head and his front legs down to reach the treat, but his hind legs will remain upright, because your other hand will prevent him from moving them. Tell him 'bow' and then give him the treat.

4 Keep practising this until he performs the movement smoothly. Then take your hand away from his stomach so that he does it on his own. When he is familiar with the word 'bow' and the movement, try the trick without the treat. Say the word 'bow' and perform a bow yourself with your hand indicating the downward movement that your dog should be adopting.

Trick 2
SPiN

This is a dance movement for dogs. Your dog will turn swiftly in a circle, spinning around as if he was chasing his tail.

2 Now slowly move your hand in a circle either to the left or right. Your dog should follow your hand.

1 Your dog begins this trick by standing perfectly still in front of you. Hold a treat or toy in your hand and raise it just above his nose.

4 Tell your dog, 'spin', and reward him. When he is familiar with this movement and is happy to perform it, try doing it without the treat or toy to lure him. Tell him to 'spin' and hold your empty hand above his nose and draw a circle above him with your hand.

5 As you practise this you can gradually increase the speed of your hand so that his circle gets faster and looks more like a spin.

Trick 3
HiGH

This trick will leave your dog standing on his hind legs for a moment or two with his legs against you. It looks very impressive but is quite easy to teach.

1 Ask your dog to stand still before you. Show your dog the treat that you hold in your left hand.

2 Now raise the treat slowly high up above his head. He will jump up towards the treat, raising himself onto his hind legs in an effort to reach it.

3 Let him put his legs against your waist so he has something to lean on. Tell him the word 'high' and reward your dog. Keep practising this trick, asking your dog to remain on his back legs for a little longer each time.

4 The next stage is to leave the dog standing on his hind legs while you turn your back to him so he rests on your back. The word is 'high' and the sign will be you raising your left hand high into the air before him.

Trick 4
WALK BACK

2 Hold a treat in your right hand in front of his nose. Take a step forwards into your dog, so encouraging him to take a step backwards. Gently press your left hand against him as a guide.

1 Ask your dog to stand in front of you, slightly to your right side.

8 Continue taking steps towards him if necessary, to guide him backwards. Reward him with the treat. Build up to more steps gradually, so that eventually he will walk backwards smoothly in front of you.

Trick 5
WALK AROUND

2 Lure your dog around your left side, keeping him close to your leg. Once he is directly in front of your body, pass the toy into your right hand.

1 Stand still with your dog sitting or standing beside you or slightly behind you. Hold a toy (or a treat) in your left hand so that he can smell it.

4 Slip the toy into your left hand again and lure your dog back in front of you. Give him the toy and praise him. He should have completed one and a half circles around you.

5 Guide him around to the right side of your body so that he has to walk behind you.

ENTERING COMPETITIONS

Gin and I really enjoyed learning new tricks in the garden and as we became more proficient I had the idea of setting some of our movements to music. The final result is what you might have seen on *Britain's Got Talent*, but that was far from the first competition Gin and I had entered.

Before appearing on the programme, we had already been pretty successful at a clutch of dog shows. At any event like this there are many different categories that people enter with their dogs, but because Gin was so good at learning new tricks I was most interested in 'Canine Freestyle'. This category gives total freedom to put anything and everything into the performance, such as tricks, jumps and spins, all matched to your choice of music.

Although we never attended any freestyle classes, after a lot of training I was satisfied that we were good enough to try a competition. And amazingly we won straight away! It was held in a sort of cattle shed and we performed a dance to the song 'Uptown Girl'. I have never had any specific ambitions, though I had always wanted to take Gin to Crufts, but since then we've won every competition we've entered.

Once you start competing at dog shows there are different stages through which to progress. That first dance was in the 'Starters' class and some people were unhappy because they felt I was too good for that section, but the rules state you must start at the bottom! After that, if you do well and win competitions then you are awarded points and you move through the ranks to 'Novice', 'Intermediate' and then 'Advanced', which is where Gin and I now compete.

GIN AND I LOVE TO COMPETE IN THESE CONTESTS, BUT IT ISN'T ALWAYS EASY

For some people it can take several years of hard work to reach the 'Advanced' level, which just shows once again how amazingly fortunate I am to have a talented dog like Gin to work with.

Each time we compete I help Gin backstage to stretch her legs to make sure she doesn't pull any muscles, just as if she were a real dancer. I suppose I should probably do a few stretches myself, but my main concern is always to make absolutely certain that Gin is properly prepared. Personally, I have never had a dance lesson in my life; I just make up the steps and try to choreograph them with Gin. Having said that, the dancers on the *Britain's Got Talent* tour have helped me learn some new steps and hopefully this will help us develop our act.

Gin and I love to compete in these contests, but it isn't always easy. While I see it as a bit of fun, others in the dog world can be rather serious in their attitude. It is a strange sport because there are so few young people involved. I'm probably about the youngest of all involved in Advanced competitions. The Kennel Club recently introduced competitions for Young Kennel Club members, under the age of 18, to encourage youngsters to compete.

Many competitors have been really impressed with our act and encourage the others to use us as a challenge to improve their own acts. I take part in this sport because I love it and I love Gin and performing with her. If you're not having fun, what's the point?

I know when I was growing up, everyone used to say to Kate and Tina: 'We can't understand why you've still got that dog.' Or: 'Why do you bother when she's so naughty and difficult?' Well, I'm an example of why it is worth persevering with the most difficult canines. But you have to be as fanatical as Kate. I think she could always see my potential. You see, the difference between me and a non-competition dog is that I don't mind doing things over and over again. Lots of dogs get bored and lose concentration. I was like that too when I was younger, but not any more. I can be under the most intense pressure now and still manage the exact same routine and still enjoy myself.

Routine is the key here and Kate is brilliant at sticking to the same routine, which calms me down and means I know what to expect. She gets up at 6.45 every morning then takes us all for a walk – all the family dogs. Among them is my really special pal Scamp. She's a little Jack Russell terrier and the newest member of our canine caucus. We got Scamp after someone tied her up and abandoned her outside the local police station. Nigel, Kate's Dad, saw her and thought he'd bring her home and contact the local warden to see if she had a chip under her skin so we could trace the owner. I took to Scamp straight away. We are both hyper together and she has this insistent sharp little bark which provokes me to play with her and we run around in circles together, which suits me just fine. We love to spar and scrap. Anyway, they couldn't trace the owner and the warden didn't want to take her to the local dog pound because it wasn't very nice, so she said: 'Why don't you take her? You've already got so many dogs – one more won't make any difference.' And that's exactly what happened. And I'm really glad because I think that Scamp understands me better than some of the other dogs who find me a bit irritating at times.

After our morning walk, we go back to our kennels to rest then Kate goes to college. I miss her when she's not here, but I have grown used to it and I love it when she comes home, because then we all go for another walk. After that, Kate and I train for an hour then there's one more walk, a dry food supper and it's bed time. It may sound a bit dull, but to me every day is a perfect day. I'm sure if Kate didn't work me quite so hard, I would become a nuisance again, just like I was when I was growing up.

I love it when Kate introduces a new move into our dance routines. It means I get a fresh treat or two – the regular work involves no extra treats – so learning something new has many incentives, not least those savoury morsels in the palm of her hand.

I think, apart from the dancing, the best days of the week are when we play Flyball. I love Flyball more than anything! Even dancing sometimes. I don't know if you've heard of it, but it is a relay race for dogs. There are six dogs per team (there are five Collies and one crossbreed in our team) and each dog has to run down a lane, jumping over four fences, catch a fly ball shot out of a box at the end and then jump the fences on the way back, then the next dog sets off. The winner is the team that completes the course in the quickest time. There's nothing like it for excitement and speed. I feel like barking at the very thought of it. And guess what? My team won the British Flyball Championship last year. High achiever? Moi? You bet!

Advanced Tricks for Dancing and Agility

Gin just loved learning all her tricks. She really likes a challenge and to use her brain! Her favourite thing is unquestionably jumping. However, it took months and months of hard, steady work to train Gin to master her advanced tricks. This chapter covers a variety of the more complicated, advanced tricks and games. When you and your dog have mastered the simple tricks, and you must learn them properly first, then you can move on to the ones shown here.

These tricks will test your dog's agility more and make him use his brain. Most dogs love to rise to a challenge and you should find that the more you ask of your dog, the more he will give you. The main thing to remember is to take everything very slowly. Don't give up when it seems to get too hard. Just give yourself and your dog a break and try again another time.

As you master more tricks and skills as a team, you will find that the bond between you grows stronger each day. After all, you'll be spending time together, learning together, having fun together and earning each other's trust. It is a very rewarding experience.

AGILITY TRAINING

The tricks described here will help your dog become more agile and nimble. Practising these moves will help him prepare for playing specific games, such as Flyball, and for agility classes and competitions.

Trick 1
ROLL OVER

To perform this trick your dog will begin by lying down and then literally roll over with his whole body as if he were rolling down a hill.

1 Command your dog to adopt the 'Flat' (see p. 54) position. If you prefer, you can position your dog on a small blanket. When he is flat, hold the treat or toy in your hand close to his nose and begin to move it in a circular movement towards the left.

2 He will begin to roll. If using a blanket, get hold of the edge nearest your dog's right side and lift it up, then gently pull it so that your dog begins to roll over.

3 Some dogs feel uncomfortable being forced onto their backs and the process may feel strange to him. So don't be disheartened if he jumps up immediately and looks unwilling to co-operate. Simply try again another time, and keep trying at different times, until he relaxes.

4 Once he lets you roll him over, practise doing it as you make the circular movement with your hand. Tell your dog 'roll over' at the same time and give him lots of praise. Eventually, the cue word will be 'roll over' with the circular movement of your hand encouraging him to roll over.

Trick 2
standing weave

For this trick your dog will weave in and out of your legs while you are standing still. Take it slowly and use plenty of treats to guide him.

1 To begin with your dog needs to be standing facing you. With a treat in your right hand, lure him through your legs.

2 Switch the treat to your left hand as he comes through and then guide him around your right leg to bring him to the front of you again.

3 Now bring him back through your legs again. Lure him around your left leg so that he eventually ends up in front of you.

4 When he's done this give him the treat and lots of praise. Tell him the word 'weave' and do the trick again.

Trick 3
BEG

For this movement your dog will raise himself onto his haunches and put his front paws in the air to make it look as though he is begging. The word for this trick is 'beg' and you can use the flat of your right hand with your palm turned upwards, moving your hand upwards a little, (as if asking someone to stand), as the sign for your dog to beg.

1 Begin this trick by asking your dog to adopt the sitting position. Now move round behind him so that you are standing close to his back.

2 Take a treat or toy in your left hand and put it just above your dog's nose. You may have to place your right hand gently but firmly on your dog's chest. This will prevent him from jumping up. Slowly raise your left hand upwards so that your dog begins to reach for the treat or toy.

3 Because you are standing behind him, he will be able to lean against your legs to help him balance. Once in the required position say 'beg' clearly and then give him a lot of praise. Eventually he should go into the begging pose without you using the treat to lure him. You should also be able to give him the cue to go into this trick while standing in front of him.

Trick 4
JUMPING OVER a stick

1 Hold a stick up for your dog to jump over. Start with it fairly low.

2 Throw a toy over the stick so that he has something to follow.

 104 Kate and Gin

3 Then, if necessary, lure him over with a treat. Move the treat over the stick and hold it on the other side.

GINFORMATION!

- *Don't attempt to teach more than one trick at a time. Otherwise you'll both get confused.*
- *Stick with your chosen cue word and sign for each trick. Write the tricks and the cues down to help you be consistent.*
- *Give yourself and your dog regular, frequent and short training sessions.*
- *Don't get frustrated with yourself or your dog.*
- *Give verbal praise with the treat. Your dog needs extra encouragement.*
- *Relax. Your dog won't perform if you're tense.*
- *Be confident and firm. Remember, you are in charge. Enjoy it!*

Trick 5
WALK BACKWARDS THROUGH LEGS

2 Straddle your legs to make an opening. Put a toy (or treat) above your dog's nose and move it backwards steadily towards you.

1 Start with your dog standing still. Place yourself behind your dog with his tail almost between your legs.

4 Whip your hand behind your back. Your dog will move through your legs and take the toy from the hand you hold behind your back.

3 Your dog should move back, following the toy.

Trick 6
CRAWL (THROUGH LEGS)

This command will have your dog crawling along the ground.

1 Ask your dog to lie 'flat' next to you. Now crouch down next to him and stretch one of your legs out in front of you so that it creates a low barrier in front of your dog.

2 Show him the toy (or treat) and get him to follow it under your leg. He will have to crawl right under your leg to get to the toy.

3 Your dog will slowly crawl under your leg towards the toy. As he does this, say the cue word 'crawl' and reward him.

4 You could use the hand sign of rolling your hands over each other to tell him to 'crawl'. Another way of teaching this is to place a broom handle on two piles of books with enough space for your dog to crawl underneath.

CRUFTS

Gin and I are serious about training, learning and improving together, but, and I have to reiterate this, the most important thing to me is that we're enjoying ourselves. If I ever believed that Gin did not love the sensation of performing then I would stop right away, but I have absolutely no doubts about her delight in dancing. Because we have so much fun I don't really set targets as such, except that ever since I was a child I have dreamed of performing at Crufts with my very own dog. It is such an amazing event, with all its great tradition and international fame and glamour, and in March of 2008 I was thrilled to be given that opportunity.

It is astonishing to look back and see how much has changed for Gin and me since the start of 2008. At that time we were still in the intermediate category of competition, appearing at Crufts was only a dream and *Britain's Got Talent* was still very much in the audition stages. Yet within a few months our lives had changed utterly.

Being offered the chance to perform at Crufts was the result of a strange set of circumstances. In February we competed in an intermediate category, doing Canine Freestyle. We were elated to win the category, which gave us enough points to move up into the advanced group. Unfortunately, this came just too late to give us a chance of competing at Crufts. I was quite happy to wait another year, but the Crufts organisers had seen our act and were so impressed that they asked us to perform in the main ring at the event, but as a demonstration rather than a competitor. It was a huge honour to be asked and of course I didn't think twice and we accepted immediately.

WE WOULD BE PERFORMING IN FRONT OF REAL DOG EXPERTS, PEOPLE WHO REALLY KNOW THEIR STUFF

Gin and I went away and made absolutely sure that the act was spot on. Even though we were not in competition, it was still incredibly nerve-wracking and extremely exciting just thinking about being in that main ring. Frighteningly, we would be performing in front of real dog experts, people who really know their stuff. That notion is so much worse than dancing in front of the general public and, I would say, even scarier than facing Simon Cowell and Piers Morgan! With the greatest respect to them, they might not spot some small errors that Gin or I might make, but at Crufts everyone would have eagle eyes!

We decided to dance to the James Bond theme, which we later reprised on *Britain's Got Talent*. We received a fantastic reception from the crowd and I was pleased to see how well Gin responded to all the clapping and cheering. Some people have asked me if Gin really enjoys this life and I really think it depends on the dog, because some dogs might easily become bored with the repetitive nature of what we do. However, Gin's enthusiasm has never faltered. She lives to be trained and I think she loves being told how great she is too! Perhaps next year we will be back at Crufts, only this time in competition!

Britain's Got Talent wasn't the first really big performance that we'd been through together. There was Crufts in Birmingham. We had to get up really early. I could tell that the event was probably the most scary to date because Kate was unusually nervous that morning. Those kinds of challenges we have faced many times now, but then I sensed that something very big was about to happen. We weren't in competition as such, but the crowds at Crufts, well, I'd never seen anything like it. And the din from all the barking and howling – the vast sound just hits the roof of the exhibition centre and reverberates around the auditorium. It is incredible. There's sawdust everywhere in case there are accidents and literally thousands of dogs are confined to tiny cubicles to await their time in the ring. I'm very glad I'm not a looker like the champions. I think it pretty likely that I would get irritated by all the primping and preening that goes on.

It is just not me at all. I'm a doer with no patience. I would be climbing the walls if I had to wait all day to trot round the ring a few times then stand there looking at the pocket of my owner for the tell-tale treat inside. I know I would blow it and do something really naughty like bark or tussle with my lead. But for the grand dance, Kate and I were second to none. A huge crowd had gathered and the performance went off without a single hitch. It set us up for *Britain's Got Talent* and was a great way of preparing for our television experience.

After we had done our routine and met all my new and adoring fans, we had time to look around a bit. It was the gun dog day and I have never seen so many extraordinary breeds. My favourites were the Italian Spinones, who look like grand old generals from some ancient British regiment, and the Clumber Spaniels. I'm told they are an endangered British breed with only a few hundred or so left. They have gorgeous white fur coats and their drooping eyes and slobbery mouths make them look like distinguished old gentlemen from some bygone era. I hope they don't go extinct. Apparently, there are quite a few endangered British breeds like that – Welsh terriers are also on the Vulnerable British Breeds list. It is a shame. I love variety, don't you? Kate said the Clumber Spaniels molted more than a yak in the summer. Maybe that is why they're not so popular anymore. At one point, I got up too close to a Chesapeake Bay Retriever and he barked ferociously at me, which made me slink away. I really don't think he behaved like a competition dog at all! And he had such amazing green eyes, which were very spooky and disconcerting. However, there are lots of wonderful dogs too and you make so many new friends.

Kate said it was a great privilege to be asked to perform at Crufts and I could see that it was. I hope we can go back. I loved it so much.

Brain Training

The exercises and tricks in this section will really help to get your dog to use his brain. By practising them regularly, your dog will be encouraged to think harder.

PROBLEM SOLVING

Gin never liked to be in one place for long. Her mind would just switch; it was like, 'oh, bored now. I'll go and find something else to do!' At obedience classes she'd be straight out of the door and running around the field! Don't expect your dog to be different....

MOTIVATING YOUR DOG

Dogs do have different personalities. They can be shy or extrovert, quiet or noisy. Some dogs like to be busy all the time, others are happy to curl up in their basket. Find out what motivates your dog.

All dogs will respond to praise. Giving your dog your attention is a definite motivator. Make sure you let your dog know when you are happy with him. You can scratch his neck or his tummy and stroke him while you give verbal praise.

Some dogs are motivated by food, others are not. Vary the treats you give your dog. You can buy lots of different kinds or make your own, but if you are giving treats, keep an eye on your dog's weight. When I'm teaching Gin new tricks I use treats, but not when we're just running through a routine.

I find that playing with Gin is the key. You build a relationship and also stamina and fitness through play. Play will build a shy dog's confidence, and help a bouncy dog to calm down if he has to wait for his play. There are many soft toys available for dogs, as well as balls and bits of rope or rubber twists to tug on. Lots of dogs are motivated by toys.

Observe your dog closely and you'll understand what motivates him – if he likes food, what kind of treat he'll do anything for, or which toy is his all-time favourite.

THE THREE MOTIVATORS
- **Praise**
- **Play**
- **Food**

TELLING HIM OFF

Of course, there are times when you need to let your dog know that he is doing something wrong. At these times a sharp 'no' is necessary. Never smack your dog. Like you, your dog will learn faster if he is praised for doing the right thing than if he is scolded for doing the wrong thing. Positive reinforcement is much more effective than negative words.

Only tell your dog off when you catch him in the act of being naughty, for example, jumping on the sofa. If you tell him off later when you actually discover the mud on the sofa, he won't understand why he is being scolded.

Never scold your dog when he comes back to you late. You must not shout at him when he does come. In your dog's mind he is being told off for obeying you. If he persists in the habit of ignoring you when you call him, then you should call him back frequently and each time praise him or give him a treat, and then send him off to play again. This way he will associate coming to you with pleasant things.

SOME COMMON PROBLEMS

Chewing

Puppies have an urge to chew. All puppies around the age of four months chew as they lose their teeth. Another teething stage begins at around eight months. Chewing his surroundings is your puppy's way of exploring the world;

and sometimes he'll just chew things out of boredom. It is up to you to show him what he can and cannot put in his mouth. If you catch him gnawing on a piece of furniture, tell him 'no' and then substitute a rubber toy like a Kong. Kongs can be stuffed with food or treats to keep him interested. When he chews the toy give him lots of praise.

Jumping Up

Puppies jump up because it is their way of saying 'hello' in an enthusiastic manner. Some people say they don't mind puppies jumping up, but a sweet puppy will soon be a fully grown dog. If your puppy jumps up then get down onto his level so that he doesn't have to jump to reach you. It is best to control your dog's tendency to jump up as soon as possible. Begin at home where you are in a quiet, controlled environment. Put your dog on the lead and sit quietly with him. Ask a friend or family member to enter the room. Encourage your dog to be quiet and to keep all four paws on the ground. If he succeeds in not jumping up, reward him. If later he forgets, ignore him until his paws are on the ground, then greet and praise him.

Persistent Barking

There are several reasons why your dog could be barking. He could be displaying territorial instincts. If this is the case, then he will bark if he thinks he hears or sees an intruder, so the barking will not be persistent. The other common reasons are loneliness or to get your attention.

Dogs are social animals, used to living in a pack. It is not natural for them to be alone for long periods of time. If you need to leave your dog alone sometimes then you should train him to tolerate isolation without fear. You can plan a programme of separation in which you leave your dog alone for just a few minutes at a time, gradually building to 30 minutes. Only continue to lengthen the amount of time you're away when your dog can cope. Before you leave the house, take no notice of him for half an hour before you go so that he gets used to being without your attention. Don't say goodbye to him or make a big fuss about collecting keys and your coat. Leave quietly. Some people put a radio on to help prevent their dog from becoming lonely.

Some dogs will bark to get your attention. In this case, don't give him any. Even a telling off is attention. Turn your back on your dog and pretend you can't hear him. You can also make a sudden loud noise like banging on a tin tray or blowing a whistle. If your dog then stops barking, praise him. When your dog stops barking get him interested in a toy or go through an exercise or trick to distract him.

Digging

It is a dog's instinct to dig. Terriers and Dachshunds dig to get at prey. German Shepherds and Huskies dig for shelter. Many dogs have the urge to bury food and some have the desire to escape. If your dog persists in digging holes in the garden, then you can try different things to discourage him.

- Limit his time alone in the garden.
- Place stones or netting over the areas he likes to dig.
- Supply other forms of entertainment, such as toys.
- Designate a small area of ground for him to dig in and encourage him to use it by praising him when he does.
- Don't let him see any family members digging in the garden. He will think it is acceptable behaviour.

GINFORMATION!

- *Observe your dog to see what motivates him. There's always a reason for a dog's behaviour.*
- *Alternate food, praise and play.*
- *Only tell your dog off when you catch him doing something naughty. Don't scold your dog if he gets a trick wrong.*
- *Positive reinforcement works best.*
- *Ignoring your dog shows him your displeasure.*
- *Distract him with a toy when he's restless.*
- *Brain Training will keep your dog alert and interested.*
- *Agility Training combined with energetic play will help to prevent your dog from developing bad habits.*

Trick 1
FiND

1 Arrange three empty containers upside down on the floor. Show your dog a delicious smelling treat and let him get its scent. Hide the treat under one of the containers.

2 Lead your dog towards the containers. Let him try and find the treat.

3 Encourage your dog to 'find' the treat. When he is smelling around the correct container, lift it up to reveal the treat, and let your dog eat the morsel of food he has found.

4 Keep practising this exercise until he gets the hang of it. Eventually, your command of 'find' will have him looking for the hidden treat immediately.

Trick 2
TARGET TRAINING

This easy trick is really an exercise that will enable you to perform other tricks with your dog. When your dog understands this command you should be able to get him to touch anything you ask him to, like your hand or your foot.

1 Put a treat on the end of a stick, or attach a small, favourite toy.

2 Hold out the stick close to your dog so that he goes to touch the end of it.

3 Say 'touch' and then take it away and feed him a treat from your hand. Don't let him eat the treat from the end of the stick.

4 Keep practising with the stick, then remove the treat and get your dog to touch the stick by using the command 'touch.' This will be useful in helping you to get your dog to perform advanced moves.

Trick 3
SIMPLE RETRIEVE OF AN OBJECT

Getting your dog to retrieve an object that you have thrown for him is the basis for many games, sports and tricks. A dog's natural instinct is to chase and catch, but not to give up! This is the part you must teach him.

1 Choose one of your dog's favourite toys and make him sit next to you.

2 Once you have his attention, throw the toy. Remember to have a treat ready.

3 Once he has the toy in his mouth, this is when you must get him to return to you. When he comes back say 'leave' or 'drop', and only when he does this should you give him a treat.

BRITAIN'S GOT TALENT: HOW IT ALL BEGAN

While we were participating in dog shows I started to consider entering *Britain's Got Talent*. I watched the series in 2007 and thought it might be fun – I quite fancied having our two minutes of fame on the telly. It would be a brand-new experience for us, plus I couldn't remember seeing a dancing dog on television before so perhaps we would have an advantage.

I checked out the *Britain's Got Talent* website and found the application form. There were a lot of questions to answer, but I didn't think we had anything to lose, so I completed it online and pressed 'send'. I waited for a couple of weeks but when no answer came I forgot that I had even applied.

Then, out of the blue, I suddenly received a letter inviting me to an audition in Manchester. I had absolutely no idea what to expect, but I did know that it was the very early days of the process, so I kept my feet on the ground and concentrated on making sure that Gin and I were ready to impress with our routine. We enjoyed the freedom to improvise – it wasn't like a dog show with a lot of rules – so I began devising a dance to really wow the producers.

This first audition was held at a hotel in Manchester, but this was just the start of the filtering process, so Amanda Holden, Simon Cowell and Piers Morgan weren't there to judge. We arrived in pouring rain and Mum had to drop us off because we couldn't find anywhere to park. As Gin and

ALL WE COULD DO WAS GO HOME AND WAIT

I walked towards the hotel all was quiet but then suddenly we turned the corner to see an enormous queue. It was pretty intimidating to see so much competition and they were queuing right around the hotel and down the road. All I could do was join the end.

The waiting began. We must have queued for over four hours. Gin was as bored as me and I began to worry that she would be totally switched off by the time it came to perform. I wasn't in the best frame of mind myself!

Finally, we made it inside the hotel where there were even more questionnaires to fill in and forms to sign. I was given a sticker with my name and number on and then sent to wait in another room, where there were hundreds of people all waiting for their opportunity to impress. Everyone seemed to be entertaining each other with singing and juggling and all sorts, partly, perhaps because of the cameras. There wasn't much room for us to limber up, though, so Gin and I sat quietly and just watched this amazing circus in front of us.

At last our names were called and we entered a room to be faced by a panel of producers and a camera to film our act. It was nerve-wracking, but after waiting so long all we could do was simply get on with it. When we finished, the producers thanked us and simply said: 'We'll get back to you.' That was it. I felt it had gone well, but we had absolutely no indication of their feelings! They might have hated us! At dog shows, you are always judged on the day, so this was a strange experience. All we could do was go home and wait...

I can honestly say that this had to be one of the most boring days of my life. I thought I was going to go nuts with the endless hanging around with nothing to do but to sit or lie down. I am sure that you have got the picture by now that I get extremely restless and even somewhat depressed when I have to wait quietly doing nothing for any length of time – let alone for most of a day! I'm quickly learning that television, however, is very much all about playing the waiting game and being patient. Hours and hours of hanging about like you're waiting for a vet's appointment, then in a poof or even a woof there's a great deal of activity and it is all over in a flash. As a *Britain's Got Talent* veteran, I now know that the key is to be able to summon the right amount of energy at exactly the right moment. I know that Kate was really anxious that I'd be completely 'switched off' by the time we got to do our routine, but now she knows that I am capable of turning it on when required. This dog certainly knows what being perky really means in showbiz and I have more professionalism in one paw than Lassie ever had in his entire body. We made the big time. No doubt about it.

Trick 4
Leave and take

1 Prepare a selection of treats. Put them in your pocket and pick up a piece of dried food. Ask your dog to get into the flat position and place a treat on his paw.

2 Put your hand between him and the treat and say 'leave' in a firm, clear voice.

3 Wait a moment with your hand still in place. Take your hand away and tell your dog 'take'. He can now eat the treat, and surprise him with an extra treat from the delicacies in your pocket. Give him lots of praise.

4 After a few sessions of this, you can try doing this exercise without the barrier of your hand. Repeat the whole process with your dog in different positions: flat, sit, stand. Then place the treat in different places, not just on his paw. Try putting it on your knee or on a chair. The aim is to get your dog to 'leave' and to 'take' on your command only.

Trick 5
Put away

1 Throw one of your dog's favourite toys (nothing too big!). He will most likely run to pick it up.

2 Often dogs don't like to give up toys or balls that they have retrieved. If you're not careful you can enter into a tug-of-war with him. Hold out a treat as an exchange and say 'drop it' clearly and firmly, and he should give up the toy. When he gives up the toy, give him the treat and praise him.

3 The next stage of this trick is to get your dog to follow you back to a container. Indicate that he should look into the container by holding a treat over it. When he is holding his head in the right position, tell him to 'drop'. Tell him to 'put your toys away' as you begin this sequence of exercises, and confirm this message when he finishes and is given his treat. Eventually, you will be able to ask him to put his toys away after you have thrown several items for him to pick up. Stand next to the container and point to the toys saying 'put your toys away.'

BRitaiN's GOt TaLENt: tHE TRiaLS

I t was agonising waiting to see whether we had made it to the next round. The first audition was in November 2007 and it wasn't until January that the letter arrived giving us the fantastic news. All kinds of emotions flowed through me. I was excited and couldn't wait, but I was also nervous, concerned that the judges might just laugh at Gin.

This round was held in a theatre and the pressure seemed even greater. Ant and Dec were backstage interviewing people, there was a huge audience and we were going to be facing the dreaded judges – Simon Cowell, Amanda Holden and Piers Morgan.

I was most scared about actually going onto the stage because I felt that our first impression would be vital. It was an anxious moment as we walked past Ant and Dec onto the stage, where Simon asked us to explain our act. When I replied, 'Canine Freestyle,' his eyebrows raised and he just said, 'OK.' He looked totally unconvinced. I think he had his finger on the rejection button already! But perhaps we had an advantage there – I don't think anyone knew what to expect and so we had that element of surprise.

This routine was set to the James Bond theme and I was really pleased with how it went. The audience loved Gin's tricks, especially when she danced backwards, and as we finished everyone was on their feet cheering and clapping, it was just unbelievable. Afterwards, when I watched it on telly, I was shocked to see Simon whisper: 'Oh. My. GOD!' He rarely seems to be impressed by anything, so that was a real compliment.

I had no idea what to expect from the judges. You can't really tell how they might react from watching them on television, but luckily they all seemed to love Gin. Amanda said: 'I'm absolutely speechless... I think he's the most talented animal I've ever seen.' That was a good start. Piers said: 'I think we've got to consider the prospect of a non-human winning *Britain's Got Talent*.' Even Simon was impressed: 'All my life I've searched for another Lassie... I think we've found one!' We were through!

I was really surprised – I had been worried about the judges' reaction and how Gin would perform with all the noise from the crowd, but she seemed to thrive on it and everything went perfectly. Backstage I had to correct Ant when he called Gin a 'he', but they were so encouraging and Ant even said it was his favourite act so far.

I wasn't allowed to tell anyone except for my parents that we were through because it was all hush hush. The next step was to go to London and stay in a hotel while the judges made their final decision as to who would make the semi-finals. At the hotel holding area the tension began to build while everyone nervously chatted and asked each other what comments they'd received from the judges. Finally, we all stood on a stage, ready to hear the results. It seemed like a decade just waiting to see if we were through, but finally they gave Gin and I the good news. I just could not believe it! I never thought they would put a dog into the semifinals, but they had. We'd done it!

IT SEEMED LIKE A DECADE JUST WAITING TO SEE IF WE WERE THROUGH

I will never forget it for as long as I can woof. It was at the end of May, a bank holiday weekend and we were staying in this hotel and I remember that they all seemed to be strangely scared of dogs and told us we couldn't go through the reception area but had to go in and out through the staff entrance at the back. They definitely wanted to keep us hidden from the rest of the guests and act as if there wasn't a dog staying in the hotel. But the one thing I don't do in this life is dwell on that kind of stuff. We had more important things to think about and a big job to focus on and I wanted, more than anything, to please Kate. And then we went to the television studio for rehearsals. I have to tell you that it was a mind-boggling experience! There were all these lights and huge lumbering cameras and cranes and jib arms and endless, endless feet of fat cables coiled in huge bundles all over the floor. At one point I looked around and hadn't a clue where we were going to perform. I knew that there was no way I was ever going to moonwalk backwards over those cables. No way. I looked at them and I started to panic, which made me pant very hard. I remember Kate reassuring me, but I was so scared that I would trip up or be blinded under those lights!

However, I managed to settle down and then we sat and watched our competition. We were there for the entire weekend and by the end of it I felt so much better. I knew everyone on the team by then and everyone was very nice to us, and they allowed Kate and I to sit in the audience and see what was going on. Eventually, I even got used to the volume of noise and I'm glad because it

was very loud in there! The time in the studio beforehand meant everything to me. I know it wouldn't have been possible for me to have just walked in and performed just like that without any preparation. Crufts was tame by comparison. Then they let me on to the stage. I didn't have to perform at first, but just walk across it once or twice and get used to the surface. It was made of some kind of hardened plastic – not too hard like concrete or too cold like metal. It yielded a little and felt warm like wood, but there was no risk of splintering – all pretty good for my fancy foot work. I'm nimble on my feet but the surface where I dance is crucial and I could feel that it was going to be OK.

Chapter Four

GETTING SERIOUS

Taking it Further

The more I train Gin the more in tune with me she becomes. After the first trick, each new trick and skill gets easier and easier to teach.

Are you ready to take things further? If so, you'll need to be confident that your dog has achieved a reliable standard of basic obedience. I strongly recommend going to obedience classes with your dog. At these classes you can consolidate what you've already taught him in a different environment, and learn new skills and commands together. It is a place to ask about any training queries you may have and to discuss tips and techniques with other owners. Also, dogs need to meet other dogs to develop their manners! You can discover where your nearest obedience class is held through the Kennel Club.

If you and your dog are enjoying your training and are keen to develop your skills, you may be interested in training your dog in one of the many sports available. There are plenty of exciting events and competitions that will test and challenge you both. Spend some time thinking about which sport or discipline would suit you and your dog. Find out as much as you can about it, then go along as a spectator to see if you like the look of the activity. Each sport or discipline demands different abilities and will need an extra enthusiastic input from you as you embark on specialised training to prepare your dog.

This section covers some of the disciplines and sports that you might like to consider. There isn't space to write about all of them as there are so many! There are, for example, breed shows (which are like beauty pageants for dogs), sledding races, working trials and gun dog trials. The Kennel Club is a good place to go for further information. The events I have chosen to include here are lots of fun and will build on the obedience training and tricks that you've already mastered.

GETTING STARTED

For most serious dog sports or competitions you will need to register your dog with the appropriate ruling canine society. The exception to this are Companion Dog Competitions, which you will find locally. At these events you can usually enter on the spur of the moment and you won't need to fill out a lot of paperwork. However, for anything else your dog must be registered. Purebreds are normally registered as puppies on the main breed register; crossbreeds and unregistered purebreds can usually be registered on a working register to allow them to take part in competitions and sports. Most official dog competitions have to be signed up for a month in advance.

Take along any equipment you might need. Have food, water and treats available for your dog, but don't feed your dog a meal immediately before competing. Don't forget your own nutrition needs as well! You'll gain energy by eating complex carbohydrates the night before. All dog shows and dog sporting events are good places for you and your dog to socialize. However, remember that your dog should be kept on the lead for safety and also have a quiet place to rest. Your dog will need time-out in his crate or in the back of the car.

Make sure that you are wearing comfortable clothes and non-slip shoes like trainers when you work with your dog in any of the sports or disciplines mentioned.

Companion Dog Shows

A Companion Dog Show is the formal name by which charity dog shows licensed by the Kennel Club are known. These fun events are run locally and have a casual feel to them. You can find them at fêtes and open days, and sometimes they are run alone as fundraising events. You can enter any of the classes on the day. One of these competitions would be an ideal place to begin competing with your dog. You'll both get the feel of performing in public but in a relaxed environment. These events are open to all breeds of dog, as well as puppies aged six months and over. Look out for the obedience classes which will have titles like 'triers', 'starters' and 'fliers'. The exercises that you will be asked to perform with your dog will be similar to the serious obedience competitions, but they won't be so strict, as they don't adhere to the Kennel Club Rules and Regulations.

Obedience Competitions

This is a popular sport and can be performed by any breed of dog. The rules and exercises usually include heelwork done on and off the lead with changes of pace. Your dog will be expected to perform a recall, to remain in the 'sit', 'stand' and 'flat' positions and to retrieve a chosen object. You will also be asked to send your dog away to a marked spot. Other requirements are scent discrimination and distance control. This event requires high levels of concentration and motivation. You will begin in a Novice class and can progress through to Advanced. The requirements for each class become harder as the levels go up.

Agility

Agility events are usually scheduled in conjunction with a traditional dog show. An agility competition is like a big obstacle race for dogs. A huge array of different equipment is set up in an arena. There are over 30 different kinds of obstacles. Expect your dog to encounter tunnels, see-saws, jumps of different heights and lengths, weave poles

and bridges, among others. These objects are chosen deliberately because they are difficult for a dog to negotiate alone; this is a real teamwork event. Your dog will rely on your encouragement and commands to get round. Leads are rarely used because they would hinder your dog's progress. You can compete as an individual or in a team.

Dog Disc Sports

The disc in question is like a Frisbee. The sport began in the early 1970s as human Frisbee sports took off and it works on a dog's natural instinct to chase, catch and retrieve. There are societies around the world now that run disc sports for dogs. The rules and classes vary according to the society that runs it. There are distance and accuracy contests, and a freestyle variation in which the game is played to music. This sport tests and develops a dog's fitness and agility. Good recall and retrieve skills are essential. In one of the games there is a timed round where teams of one dog and one thrower attempt to make as many successful throws and catches as they can before a minute is up. Extra points are gained for more complicated and longer throw-and-catch combinations. You will need to practise your own throwing skills as well as training your dog to catch the disc in mid air and return it to you.

HEELWORK TO MUSIC

This really is dancing with dogs! Gin loves this event. In these competitions, the dog works off the lead on the left and right side of the handler. The main criteria is that the dog keeps in close and has constant contact with its owner. In some competitions, particularly Freestyle, the dog is allowed to break away from his owner to perform other movements, but heelwork is much less a part of the routine. Routines are usually fairly fast. Each routine lasts four minutes and you will have chosen your own music and worked on the choreography in advance, so that you and your dog will have had the opportunity to train thoroughly before the event. The marking of a routine is divided into three categories: Programme Content (the variety of moves included), Accuracy and Execution of Movement and Musical Interpretation.

TRAVELLING TO COMPETITIONS AND EVENTS

If you and your dog become seriously involved in a sport or discipline, it is likely that you will need to travel to events. If your dog is to be transported regularly in the car, then it is vital that you should make sure that he is as safe and comfortable as possible.

At the very least, a dog guard should be fitted behind the seat to prevent your dog from distracting the driver. However, travel crates in the back of the car will keep your dog safer. Some models of car have their own rigid cases custom-made for the car. These tend to be too heavy to lift in and out frequently and so remain in the car. Make your dog's crate cosy with a newspaper lining and a blanket. Another option is to acquire a special dog harness to be used in the car. These harnesses are attached to the seat belt. Some points to remember when transporting your dog:

- Make sure your dog has been encouraged to relieve himself before getting into the car.
- Don't give solid food just before a journey.
- Take water with you in a travel container.
- Train your dog to remain inside the car until you give him the command to jump out.
- Never leave your dog in a car without leaving a window open for air. Even in the winter the temperature can rise quickly in a sealed car.

GINFORMATION!

- *Achieve a good level of obedience first.*
- *Do your research. Check out an event as a spectator to see what's required.*
- *Start to train your dog with your chosen sport in mind.*
- *Make sure your dog is registered. Sign up for competitions in advance.*
- *Give yourself plenty of time to practise.*
- *Attend to your dog's safety and comfort in the car and at the event.*
- *Have fun! Stay as relaxed as possible; dogs sense tension.*
- *Have a secure place (like a crate) where your dog can rest.*

BRITAIN'S GOT TALENT: THE SEMIFINALS

If I thought the pressure had been tough in the first few rounds, it was nothing compared to the wait for the semi-finals! This is the time where everyone dares to believe they have a chance to win, and the possibility of performing at the Royal Variety Show is tantalisingly close.

I was keen to show the judges that we had more in our arsenal, so, using the weeks to prepare, we began forming a brand-new routine. We decided to use 'I Don't Feel Like Dancing' by the Scissor Sisters as our new music and I started thinking about a new costume for the performance.

The semifinal was in London and we were put up in a hotel for four days over the May bank holiday weekend in preparation for the Monday broadcast. It was daunting, because this was a different stage with bright flashing lights and a lot of cameras, so it was difficult for me and especially for Gin to adapt. I was completely confident in the routine because of our extremely thorough preparation, but all these different elements gave me a few doubts. Fortunately, the production team allowed us to spend some time in the studio over the weekend and gradually Gin became used to the strange environment.

The build-up was tense with all kinds of worries about hair, make-up and costume, and all the acts were really nervous. Although, strangely, by the time the semifinal arrived Gin and I were totally calm. We had done so many rehearsals

that day that when it finally came to the live event it simply felt like another rehearsal. Also, the audience were fantastic and really supportive, which helped enormously.

The entire routine worked beautifully and once again all the judges were really positive and appreciative. Piers said Gin was the most talented dog in the world, while Simon wondered if Gin was really a human in a dog suit! Over those few days all the acts had mingled and we had become good friends, so it was a difficult time knowing that only two of us were going through to the final despite the fact that they were all unbelievably talented. I was desperate to take that last step – if we could go that far then we would go on the *Britain's Got Talent* tour and I knew that would be a wonderful opportunity and a great experience.

tHe auDience weRe fantastic anD ReaLLy suPPoRtive

Back on stage, we waited anxiously for the results. Signature won the public vote, so they were through and the judges were left to decide between Dean Wilson and us. I was sure they would prefer Dean, a singer, rather than an animal act like ours. Piers praised us, but chose to vote for Dean. I was convinced that was it and we were going home. But then Simon levelled the score: 'I like originality and I happen to love animals.' It was down to Amanda. She couldn't seem to make up her mind, but eventually she said: 'I'm not going to break two hearts, I'm sending Kate and Gin through!' It was such an amazing moment! I looked down at Gin, her eyes were shining and I could tell that she knew exactly what was going on. I couldn't believe I was going to the final – it was such a fantastic feeling. I hugged Gin. A dream come true.

I knew when the actual day of the semifinal was coming. Everyone was behaving differently. They sat Kate down in a chair and I watched as they transformed her from the lovely fresh-faced girl from Cheshire that I had known since I was a puppy into a television celebrity with lots of paint and colours around her eyes and glitter. They call it glamorous. I call it camouflage. Something to hide behind. I barely recognized Kate with all that make up on! I have to admit that she did look glamorous though, but I'm glad my face is too hairy to have to put any of that stuff on.

The performance in the end was a complete triumph. I couldn't believe the reaction of the crowd. It was deafening and almost frightening. Then the judges were all giving us the big thumbs up and saying lovely things to me and Kate. Just like a champagne bubble it did all go straight to my head, but hey, we were good, so why not?

Afterwards we went to some party and Kate was talking to people but I was done for. It was like my strength had evaporated. I'd given it my all and I wanted to go back to the hotel and go to sleep in my special foam bed. But after all that effort a couple of London cabbies refused to take me in their taxi! I mean, I wanted to ask: 'Do you know who I am?' A star in the firmament of British variety! Later, we hailed another taxi and the driver actually recognized me, if you can believe it, but not only that, he refused to take any money saying that we had given him and his wife so much pleasure over the last few weeks that he didn't want to charge a fare. So they're not all bad.

BRITAIN'S GOT TALENT: THE FINAL AND THE AFTERMATH

I was overjoyed to be in the final of *Britain's Got Talent*. But we had a problem that was shared by a lot of the acts on the bill. Prior to this stage, we had put everything into ensuring that we were perfect for the semifinal – all our concentration, all our efforts were focused on that event. Then suddenly we were through to the final with virtually no time at all to compose or prepare ourselves.

We stayed in London until the big day, doing more rehearsals and once again making decisions regarding music and costume. My idea was to return to our original James Bond theme routine but with some new moves that would surprise the audience and the judges. It wasn't easy. Gin had learnt the dance so immaculately for the semifinal that she began to get confused when we started trying to practise the old routine again. It was a bit of a rush job, but I think Gin pulled it off. Maybe the emotion of the occasion carried us through and I absolutely loved that last performance.

The routine brought the audience to their feet once more and I could tell Gin was beginning to love the attention and adulation. Ant and Dec asked me how it went and commented that Gin was the most famous dog in Britain, which was a weird feeling. Once again all the judges were

AT THAT POINT, I HONESTLY DIDN'T CARE IF WE WON OR NOT

very kind and encouraging. Piers was funny, saying: 'I've never even seen Michael Jackson do a backwards 360 degree moonwalk dance.' Amanda remarked that we were a world-class act, and Simon said: 'I really hope Britain gets behind you, this is one unique act.' At that point, I honestly didn't care if we won or not – I wanted to of course – but simply being in the final, experiencing the crowds and hearing that sort of praise from the judges was more than I ever could have wished for.

Ultimately, George Sampson deservedly won for his fabulous dancing act. Since then we've been on this wonderful tour and all of us have become close friends. There has been a lot of press attention, which we've had to get used to ever since the *Britain's Got Talent* cameras took over our house for the day to film me and Gin, but we have tried to take it in our stride.

We performed at the O2 Arena in front of over 6,000 people and even I'm surprised how well Gin danced under that sort of pressure. She's learnt the music perfectly and the only thing that shakes her concentration now is at the end of the dance when the audience start to scream. The noise they make, especially for George Sampson, is deafening, but I have to admit I find it pretty exciting when the audience are screaming at me! Apparently the tour managers have said that they've worked on all kinds of boy band tours over the years and they've never seen anything like the reaction the *Britain's Got Talent* tour received.

Gin gives me the confidence to go up on the stage each night and perform. I think a lot of dogs can be taught tricks and to dance, but not every dog could deal with the lights, the noise and the screaming, yet Gin seems to love it more each time. It's been a beautiful adventure, but perhaps this is only the beginning.

What a roller coaster it has been! And maybe, like Kate says, this is just the beginning. There's a lot to cope with; the fans waiting at the door, the chauffeur-driven cars, the savoury treats and stuffed toys that await me in the dressing room. But like I said in the beginning, I'm no diva. Yet...

However, all the fanfare and the razzmatazz in the showbiz firmament means nothing to me without Kate. She is my rock, the one who has made me what I am today and she is the one who will go on loving me when the lights have dimmed.

If there's one thing that I really don't like in this whole escapade, it's the screaming. For some reason our show brings out the scream in everyone. Particularly our act. For me, shouting is OK, that's no problem. It has a lower decibel. Clapping is also OK. It has a different impact on a dog's ear. But the screaming seems to hit my ears at a pitch that is far too high for comfort. When you hear dogs wailing at sirens or other high-pitched sounds, we're not singing, we're in pain! Noises like that make our ears hurt. I now know the last bars of the music before the screaming starts and as far as I'm concerned it's my cue to get off stage and the quicker the better. Sorry, but there it is. I don't mean to be rude or that I don't appreciate the audience's reaction, but it hurts too much! So if you're coming to see us as at any time (we're up for appearing in a panto in Windsor at Christmas) and I hope you are, please spare a thought for my ears. Applause is more than enough for me.

If there are any other dogs out there who are wondering if they should be venturing out into the talent show circuit, all I can say is read about my experiences and how to do it in this book, and if you're still keen, give it a go, but don't expect a cake walk. Get ready for the moonwalk! Woof! Woof!

THE FUTURE

A great deal has changed in my life in the last year. When I consider that only a few months ago virtually no one knew me or Gin and now we have appeared on television and are asked to perform in front of thousands of people I feel like I have to pinch myself.

After the *Britain's Got Talent* tour finished Gin and I spent the summer performing all over the country at various arenas, holiday camps and theatres, and we loved every minute. We've also been given the opportunity to appear in panto in Windsor over Christmas, which promises to be a unique and fun experience.

I'm now at an age where I do need to start thinking about my future and I'm fortunate that this last year has given me a base to build on. My immediate goal is to finish college and my animal management course. After that I would love to move on and train more animals, specifically for television and film. Although I've enjoyed being on stage with Gin, I don't really feel that's where my long-term future lies. My relationship with Gin has been so fulfilling and given me so much happiness, and I would love the chance to continue to train animals for the rest of my life.

Useful Information

Contacts

Animal Samaritans
PO Box 154
Bexleyheath
Kent
DA16 2WS
t: 020 8303 1859
www.animalsamaritans.org.
co.uk

Association of Pet
Behaviour Counsellors
PO Box 46
Worcester WR8 9YS
www.apbc.org.uk

Association of Pet Dog
Trainers (APDT)
PO Box 17
Kempsford
GL7 4WZ
t: 01285 810811
www.apdt.co.uk

Battersea Dogs' Home
4 Battersea Park Road
London SW8 4AA
t: 020 7622 3626
www.dogshome.org.uk

British Veterinary
Association
7 Mansfield Street

London W1G 9NQ
t: 020 7636 6541
www.bva.co.uk

Burns Dog Food
T: 0800 083 66 96
www.burns-pet-nutrition.
co.uk

Canine Concepts
www.canineconcepts.co.uk

Pet Planet
www.petplanet.co.uk

Puppy School
PO Box 186
Chipping Norton
Oxon OX7 3XG
www.puppyschool.co.uk

RSPCA
t: 0870 55 55 999 for
24-hour national cruelty
and advice line
t: 0870 33 35 999 to
register for enquiries
service
www.RSPCA.org.uk

The Kennel Club
1-5 Clarges Street
Piccadilly
London

W1J 8AB
t: 0870 606 6750
f: 020 7518 1058
www.thekennelclub.org.uk

The Wag and Bone Show
www.wagandboneshow.
co.uk

Magazines

Dog World
t: 01233 621877
www.dogworld.co.uk

Dogs Monthly
t: 0870 730 8433
www.dogsmonthly.co.uk

Dogs Today
t: 01276 858860
www.dogstodaymagazine.
co.uk

Our Dogs
t: 0161 236 2660
www.ourdogs.co.uk

Your Dog BPG (Stamford)
Ltd
t: 01780 766199
www.yourdog.co.uk

Acknowledgements

Many thanks to all the people that have made this book possible:

Firstly thanks to Carole & Stuart Thornley of Aricia Dog Training who helped with Gin's puppy socialisation and basic obedience. Without your kind patience and help Gin and I would not have been able to achieve so much.

The Young Kennel Club who introduced the various dog sports to us at the four summer camps we attended.

Live Wires Flyball Club (Warrington) for enabling us to excel in this fun and exciting sport.

The *Britain's Got Talent* team who made our journey from audition to the live finals an enjoyable and exciting experience. Thanks to Simon Cowell, Amanda Holden, Piers Morgan and Ant and Dec for believing in us and giving us the confidence to carry on.

The 2008 *Britain's Got Talent* Tour team, managed by Tony Harpur. Stephen Mulhern with his introductions and requests to the audience not to scream and cheer during Gin's performance. To all the finalists for becoming good friends and allowing Gin to become the Tour Bus pet.

To Reaseheath College (where I study Animal Management) for being so understanding, allowing us to train in the Sports Hall and letting us take photos on the premises. Thanks to Richard Palmer and Simon Walton for the photography.

To Claire Kingston and the HarperCollins Publishing team, without whom this great book would not exist.

To Mark Cowan of Creative Entertainment Group (Agents) for all his help and assistance.

Jari pet jewellery for the beautiful silver jewelled collar and matching choker that Gin and I are wearing in the book.

And finally to my very supportive family who have helped and encouraged me throughout the last 16 years. I will always be indebted to them for choosing Gin as my first dog and best friend.

Index

If you have enjoyed this book, why not learn more about 'man's best friend' with other Collins titles?

Puppy Handbook
978-0-00-714264-4
128pp PB
£7.99

Dog Training Handbook
978-0-00-711155-8
128pp PB
£7.99

Collins Need to Know? Dog Breeds
978-0-00-726854-2
192pp PB
£9.99

Dogs Behaving Badly
978-0-00-724437-9
128pp PB
£7.99

Collins Dog Owner's Guide
[128 pp | PB | £8.99]
series includes:

Border Collie
978-0-00-727429-1

Staffordshire Bull Terrier
978-0-00-727428-4

Cavalier King Charles Spaniel
978-0-00-727431-4

Jack Russell Terrier
978-0-00-727430-7

Boxer
978-0-00-721664-2

Labrador
978-0-00-717832-2

Cocker Spaniel
978-0-00-717607-6

West Highland White Terrier
978-0-00-717831-5

English Springer Spaniel
978-0-00-717605-2

German Shepherd
978-0-00-717833-9

Yorkshire Terrier
978-0-00-717606-9